MERCURY RISING

CRITICAL ISSUES TOO HOT TO HANDLE

DR. JAY STRACK

AND

DR. RICHARD LAND

NELSON IMPACT
A Division of Thomas Nelson Publishers
Since 1798

www.thomasnelson.com

Published by Nelson Impact, a Division of Thomas Nelson, Inc., P.O. Box 141000, Nashville, TN 37214.

All Scripture quotations are taken from *The New King James Version*.® (NKJV®) Copyright © 1982 by Thomas Nelson, Inc. Used by permission. All rights reserved.

ISBN: 1-4185-0592-7

Printed in the United States of America

06 07 08 09 RRD 9 8 7 6 5 4 3 2 1

Page design by Crosslin Creative
2743 Douglas Lane, Thompsons Station, Tennessee 37179

CONTENTS

INTRODUCTION

Philosophers call it the *philosophy of life.*

A psychology professor once said it is our *reason for being.*

History teachers speak of understanding *history's significance upon mankind.*

You and I know the dilemma too well, often wondering, *Who am I? Why am I here? Where am I headed?*

In an effort to resolve these probing, universal questions, our culture bombards us with various views, opinions, and belief systems that sometimes seem to answer these questions. But too often, these multiple views and philosophies collide with the truths of the Judeo-Christian worldview, which are plainly taught throughout the pages of the Bible.

In light of what we hear and read daily, it seems strange that any Christian would not recognize the need to understand and be able to correctly defend a sure and true Christian worldview. As followers of Jesus Christ, it is our privilege and our responsibility to *know what we believe and why.*

Our worldview is the perspective through which we look at people, cultural issues, and our responsibilities. Our worldview affects how we process decisions and what we believe about important issues. It is the baseline we use for interpreting our reality and establishing priorities.

In our experience, we believe that it is only when we establish a Christian worldview can we live the life that we have always wanted. Just as a correct prescription for glasses or contacts puts the world into clearer focus for your eyes, a correct biblical worldview will do the same for your life.

The lessons in this study guide are designed with you in mind— to help you as you are daily confronted with competing and conflicting worldviews. In *Mercury Rising*, we will dig deep into eight controversial and significant issues. These topics have been described by some as "too hot to handle," but if Christian students do not understand these issues correctly and meet them head-on, this generation is headed for a meltdown.

Join us as we explore both the compassion and the influence of Jesus Christ in the areas of abortion, euthanasia, cloning, pornography, sexual promiscuity, homosexuality, war, and responsible citizenship. Our goal is to help you think and act responsibly, or in a popular term, to think and act "Christianly." Our Christian worldview must not only be correctly based on Scripture, but it must also include compassion and love for others. This study guide will equip you to do just that.

KEY

STUDENT LEADERSHIP UNIVERSITY CURRICULUM

Throughout this study guide, you will see several icons or headings that represent an idea, a statement, or a question that we want you to consider as you experience Scripture in this study guide series. Refer to the descriptions below to help you remember what the icons and headings mean.

transfuse (trans FYOOZ)ː to cause to pass from one to another; transmit

The goal of the lesson for the week.

Experience Scripture: Learning to really experience Scripture is the key element to "getting" who God is and all that He has in store for you.

infuse (in FYOOZ)ː to cause to be permeated with something (as a principle or quality) that alters usually for the better

Through journaling, group discussion, and personal study, experience Scripture as it permeates your heart and alters your life.

Future Tense Living: Your choices today will determine your future. Learn how to live with dynamic purpose and influence.

Attitude Reloaded: Rethink your attitude! Learn to replace self-centered, negative, or limited thoughts with positive, courageous, compassionate thoughts that are based on God's unlimited ability and power.

 In His Steps: Every attitude and action of your life should begin with the questions, How would Jesus respond to this person and situation before me? What would He choose to do?

diffuse (di FYOOZ), to pour out and permit or cause to spread freely; to extend, scatter

Once God's Word is infused into your heart, it will pour forth to others without restraint. In this section, explore what that looks like in your daily life.

 Called to Lead: Learn how to lead others as Christ would.

 Called to Stand: Know what you believe and learn how to defend it with clarity and strength.

Called to Share: Sharing truth and serving others are results of a transformed life. How can you share with others the awesome things you're learning?

One Thing: Consider ONE THING you can do this week to make a difference in your life and/or the life of another.

[FUSE BOX]

Power up for the week with this focused truth.

CHAPTER 1

ABORTION:
WHEN DOES LIFE BEGIN?

KEY SCRIPTURE

My frame was not hidden from You, when I was made in secret, and skillfully wrought in the lowest parts of the earth. Your eyes saw my substance, being yet unformed. And in Your book they all were written, the days fashioned for me, when as yet there were none of them.

—Psalm 139:15–16

IN THE NEWS

"My name is Gianna Jessen. I am adopted. I have cerebral palsy. My biological mother was 17 years old and seven and one-half months pregnant when she made the decision to have a saline abortion. I am the person she aborted. I lived instead of died.

"Fortunately for me the abortionist was not in the clinic when I arrived alive, instead of dead, at 6:00 a.m. I was early, my death was not expected to be seen until about 9 a.m., when he would probably be arriving for his office hours. I am sure I would not be here today if the abortionist would have been in the clinic as his job is to take life, not sustain it. Some have said I am a 'botched abortion', a result of a job not well done.

> And the LORD God formed man of the dust of the ground, and breathed into his nostrils the breath of life; and man became a living being.
> —Genesis 2:7

"There were many witnesses to my entry into this world. My biological mother and other young girls in the clinic, who also awaited the death of their babies, were the first to greet me. I am told this was a hysterical moment. Next was a staff nurse who apparently called emergency medical services and had me transferred to a hospital.

"I remained in the hospital for almost three months. There was not much hope for me in the beginning. I weighed only two pounds. A doctor once said I had a great will to live and that I fought for my life. I eventually was able to leave the hospital and be placed in foster care. I was diagnosed with cerebral palsy as a result of the abortion.

"My foster mother was told that it was doubtful that I would ever crawl or walk. I could not sit up independently. Through the prayers and dedication of my foster mother, and later many other people, I eventually learned to sit up, crawl, then stand. I walked with leg braces and a walker shortly before I turned age four. I was legally adopt-

Dr. William Frist, world-renowned heart-lung transplant surgeon and prominent senator, declared on the floor of the U.S. Senate (July 29, 2005):

> I believe human life begins at conception. It is at this moment that the organism is complete—yes, immature—but complete. An embryo is nascent human life. It's genetically distinct. And it's biologically human. It's living. This position is consistent with my faith. But to me, it isn't just a matter of faith. It's a faith of science. Our development is a continuous process—gradual and chronological. We were all once embryos. The embryo is human life at its earliest stage of development. And *accordingly, the human embryo has moral significance and moral worth. It deserves to be treated with the utmost dignity and respect* (italics added).

Dr. Frist has clearly stated the compelling case for why abortion, the taking of a human life, must never be done merely because a pregnancy is embarrassing, expensive, ill, or inconvenient.

dominion over the fish of the sea, over the birds of the air, and over the cattle, over all the earth and over every creeping thing that creeps on the earth'" (Genesis 1:26).

✦ *Humans are the crowning glory of God's creation.* "So God created man in His own image; in the image of God He created him; male and female He created them" (Genesis 1:27).

✦ *Humans are the only beings to receive the "breath of life" from God.* "And the LORD God formed man of the dust of the ground, and breathed into his nostrils the breath of life; and man became a living being" (Genesis 2:7).

infuse (in FYOOZ): to cause to be permeated with something (as a principle or quality) that alters usually for the better

Consider your own unique creation in God's image:

✦ *I am created in the image of God.*

✦ *I have God-breathed life.*

Wow—it's amazing just to say it, isn't it?

 When you meditate on these amazing thoughts, does it cause you to think of yourself differently?

_____

_____

_____

✦ Human beings are the only spiritual-physical beings in God's creation.

+ Only human beings are created with the God-given capacity for spiritual fellowship with and worship of the Creator.

+ God's Spirit only fills human beings.

The Bible tells us that children are a gift through which God blesses each succeeding generation:

+ "Behold, children are a heritage from the LORD, the fruit of the womb is a reward" (Psalm 127:3).

+ "Now Adam knew Eve his wife, and she conceived and bore Cain, and said, 'I have acquired a man from the LORD'" (Genesis 4:1).

+ "And [Esau] lifted his eyes and saw the women and children, and said, 'Who are these with you?' So [Jacob] said, 'The children whom God has graciously given your servant'" (Genesis 33:5).

Have you ever thought of yourself as a *reward* to your parents? They might be wondering what they did to receive such a reward! How should this understanding affect your behavior and family life?

When you think of God's Word, what comes to mind? In the below list, check all that apply and add one or two of your own:

❏ instruction

❏ rules

❏ judgment

❏ encouragement

❏ help

❏ hope

❏ truth

❏ boring

❏ interesting

❏ other: _____

If God created you in His image and with His own breath, then don't you imagine that He wants the best for you? His judgments and laws are for your good.

diffuse (di FYOOZ); to pour out and permit or cause to spread freely; to extend, scatter

When Does Human Life Begin?
The debate in our culture and in our government roars on as to when life begins. *The final word must belong to the One who created life.* Only He really knows, and He is talking:

- ✦ *God's involvement in an individual's human conception begins in the womb.* "Thus says the Lord, your Redeemer, and He who formed you from the womb: 'I am the LORD who makes all things'" (Isaiah 44:24).

- ✦ *God ordains a unique life purpose while a human is in the womb.* "Before I formed you in the womb I knew you; before you were born I sanctified you; I ordained you a prophet to the nations" (Jeremiah 1:5).

- ✦ *Each unborn child is uniquely and carefully formed by God.* "For You formed my inward parts; You covered me in my mother's womb" (Psalm 139:13).

✦ *With detailed preparation, planning, and participation, God gives the unborn child specific personal attributes.* "Your eyes saw my substance, being yet unformed. And in Your book they all were written, the days fashioned for me, when as yet there were none of them" (Psalm 139:16).

✦ *God's personal involvement in a person's life begins in the womb.* "For he [John the Baptist] will be great in the sight of the Lord, and shall drink neither wine nor strong drink. He will also be filled with the Holy Spirit, even from his mother's womb" (Luke 1:15).

What About the "Morning-After Pill"?

The morning-after pill works by blocking implantation of a tiny embryo in the uterine wall after conception. In such a case, an abortion occurs because a life has been conceived but medically prevented from continued development. "Many women will buy the lie that they are actually preventing pregnancy, when in reality, in many cases, all they will have done is terminate a very early pregnancy, an abortion in other words," Barrett Duke, the Southern Baptist's Ethics & Religious Liberty Commission vice president for public policy, has said.[6]

> For as [a person] thinks in his heart, so is he.
> —Proverbs 23:7

True, taking a pill does seem easy and without consequence. In fact, the greatest danger of the morning-after pill may be the temptation for women to keep taking it without regard to the number of babies who are killed, because it seems to have no consequence.

Many women reason that if they kill their babies by taking the morning-after pill before they know they have conceived, then there is no harm done. If they can't prove there was a baby, they think, they can't prove there was an abortion.

GROUP DISCUSSION

Which of the statements above:

Is the most potent argument for life at conception?

_____

_____

_____

Stands out to you as very important in this debate?

_____

_____

_____

You have heard that God has a future planned for you. Did you know that God planned your future from the moment you were conceived? How should this astounding truth affect your daily choices?

_____It does matter how you act.

_____It does matter what you choose to do.

_____You do have a unique purpose and call on your life.

These Scripture passages plainly reveal that from the moment of conception, God is creating a new and unique individual. These are absolute truths that you must know if you are to accurately and clearly explain that life begins at conception.

♦ *The Bible makes no distinction between the humanity and personhood of the unborn and the born.* "For indeed, as soon as the voice of your greeting sounded in my ears, the babe leaped in my womb for joy" (Luke 1:44).

Mary visited Elizabeth, her cousin, who was six months pregnant with John the Baptist. As Mary shared the joyous news of the Messiah's coming arrival, Elizabeth's babe responded by leaping in her womb.

The Greek word used in Luke 1:44 for "babe" is *brephos*. The same word is used:

♦ To describe Jesus in the manger (Luke 2:16)

♦ To describe Timothy as a "child" learning the Scriptures (2 Timothy 3:15).

Science has now confirmed what the Bible has always revealed—life begins at conception. What has been asserted as a faith affirmation from the Bible is now confirmed as scientific fact. Dr. Bernard Nathanson, formerly the head of one of the largest abortion clinics, has said that the scientific disciplines of embryology and fetalogy "make it undeniably evident that life begins at conception and requires all the protection and safeguards that any of us enjoy."

Are There Any Exceptions?

The taking of human life can only be defended when it is the only way to protect another human life—namely, in the case that a mother will die if her pregnancy continues. This is an extremely rare circumstance in a medically-advanced country like the United States.

Twenty-two times the Scripture speaks of God's *truth* and *mercy* in the same verse. When we stand on truth, we must not neglect to show the mercy of God to those who have chosen abortion. Christ has died for their sin, and He is willing to forgive and restore.

What Do I Do If I Have a Pregnant Friend?[7]

L isten—we speak the loudest by listening (Ecclesiastes 3:7)

I nvest—in her and the baby's life with love (Proverbs 3:3)

F ocus—on her problem with patience (Proverbs 14:29)

E nsure—that she knows the Lord (Matthew 11:28–29)

What If I Am Pregnant?

✦ *Remember that God's love for you and your baby is unchangeable.* His complete forgiveness covers any sin. God offers you the power to face life, to complete your decision, and to live a wonderful future.

✦ *Go to your parents, God's protection and authority in your life.* They love you, and they will be there for you. If you honestly cannot go to your parents alone, contact your youth minister or pastor.

✦ *Contact a Christian pregnancy center* that will help you with counseling, Bible study, parenting advice, and physical needs for you and your baby. Take your parents with you for counseling as you consider the options: to keep the baby or give it up for adoption.

What If Someone I Know Already Had an Abortion?
Take her to the nearest Christian pregnancy center for professional help, and assure her of God's unconditional love.

What is ONE THING you can do this week to be ready to help a person who is pregnant to make the decision against abortion?

_____ Find a Christian pregnancy center in your area.

_____ Volunteer at a local pregnancy center.

_____ Know by heart at least two Scriptures about God's involvement with life at conception.

FUSE BOX

Science is not proof of the Bible, but the Bible proves the truth in science. The truth of Scripture is enough to live by.

NOTES

Chris was fifteen when she heard her pastor say, "Find *one thing* this week you can do to make a difference in a life." She saw an ad in the pew for the local pregnancy center and decided to volunteer. She went in and offered to babysit and fold clothes, but she was asked to go through counseling training instead. At sixteen, Chris led a single mom to Christ as the young woman made the decision to keep her baby. It so thrilled her that she went on to get a master's degree in crisis counseling, and she now serves in ministry today. One day can make a difference in your life as well as the life of a young mom!

PRIVATE WORLD DEVOTIONS

MONDAY: See it. Read the surrounding passages or chapter for the Key Scripture so that you can get an understanding of the background and context. This helps you to really *see* the verse.

TUESDAY: Hear it. Read the daily Key Scripture and/or surrounding passage out loud, putting your name in, if applicable. For example, <u>John</u> *can do all things through Christ. Thieves have come to destroy* <u>John</u>, *but Jesus has come that* <u>John</u> *might have eternal life.*

WEDNESDAY: Write it. Write the verse and then what it says about:

- ✦ *Others:* Respond, serve, and love as Jesus would.
- ✦ *Me:* Specific attitudes, choices, or habits.
- ✦ *God:* His love, mercy, holiness, peace, joy, etc.

PRIVATE WORLD JOURNAL

I am grateful for—I praise You for—I am feeling—I am thinking—I need help with

PRIVATE WORLD DEVOTIONS *(Continued)*

THURSDAY: Memorize it. Take the verse with you—write it on a card or put it in your phone, iPod, or PDA. Go over it throughout the day so that it begins to *live* in your heart and mind.

FRIDAY: Pray it. Personalize the verse as you pray for yourself or for others or in praise to God. To pray is literally "to think about." Try thinking out loud or writing in your **PRIVATE WORLD JOURNAL.**

SATURDAY: Share it. Ask the Lord to bring someone to mind or in your path today who needs good news. Don't be shy—just let it out! Whether you IM, write, text, tell, or send it, the joy of God's Word will flow from your heart into theirs.

PRAYER REQUESTS

Date	Name	Need	Answer

PRIVATE WORLD JOURNAL

I am grateful for—I praise You for—I am feeling—I am thinking—I need help with

NOTES

CHAPTER 2

MERCY KILLING:
DEATH ON DEMAND?

KEY SCRIPTURE

It is appointed for men to die once,
but after this the judgment.
—Hebrews 9:27

IN THE NEWS

On April 9, 1982, a woman in Bloomington, Indiana, gave birth to a son who was quickly diagnosed with Down syndrome, a chromosomal abnormality that produces mental retardation. The little boy, soon to be known as Baby Doe, also had esophageal atresia (the separation of the esophagus from the stomach), which made it impossible for him to ingest food.

The obstetrician who delivered the baby told the parents that their baby would have only a 50 percent chance of surviving surgery to correct the digestive problem, and that even if they were successful, the baby boy would remain significantly mentally handicapped and would have a lifetime of disability and dependency. This doctor advised the parents to withhold treatment and let their child die.

In light of the recent tragedy of the Terri Schiavo case, the administration of basic hydration and nutrition through a feeding tube to a comatose patient should *never* be considered an extraordinary means that can morally be removed. As the late Pope John Paul II put it, the removal of a feeding tube is "euthanasia by omission."

Two other doctors, who remained true to their healing profession—a hospital pediatrician and the family's physician—both disagreed vehemently with the first doctor's advice and called for immediate surgery. Tragically, the parents decided they did not want their infant son treated.

So Baby Doe was shunted aside into a darkened room with instructions to be given no water or nutrients via intravenous drugs. This decision was upheld by the Indiana Supreme Court as a "quality of life" decision—a decision that caused Baby Doe to die of thirst and starvation on April 15, 1982.[1]

IT'S TRUE!

+ A computer program exists that allows a person to click "yes" for three questions in order to activate a syringe driver with lethal drugs for the purpose of suicide. The "Self Deliverance" program was offered over the Internet as a free download.[2]

+ A physician has announced that he will conduct workshops where participants would use an on-site laboratory to make their own "peaceful pill." He says, "They drink it and go to sleep and quickly die."[3]

transfuse (trans FYOOZ): to cause to pass from one to another; transmit

Euthanasia is the *intentional killing* by act or omission of a dependent human being for his or her *alleged* benefit.[4] The drive to promote a quality-of-life ethic over a sanctity-of-life ethic is the supposed justification for euthanasia, or mercy killing. Those who promote such have begun to label:

+ Handicapped babies as disposable.

◆ The weak and the elderly as a "nuisance" and "burden to others."

Euthanasia and assisted-suicide advocates continue to push their agenda throughout the world to make death-on-demand acceptable and legal. In an interview with London's *Sunday Times*, Britain's leading medical ethics expert, Dr. Warnock, stated that it is better for elderly people to kill themselves than to be a burden on their families and society. "I don't see what is so horrible about the motive of not wanting to be an increasing nuisance," she said. In Dr. Warnock's view, only productive, independent people have value. All others are a "nuisance."[5]

Anyone who has ever had a loving, precious grandparent or an elderly friend is shocked by such a harsh statement! It's unthinkable to say that a person whose life has been a gift to family and created and treasured by God would suddenly be labeled as *disposable*. And those of us who believe in God's supreme control and creative design of all people are horrified when we hear about:

◆ Killing the elderly instead of waiting for God's timing of natural death.

◆ Disposing of babies created by God who don't "measure up."

When people look back on the tragic case of Terri Schiavo, they should remember that while she was either in a Persistent Vegetative State (PVS) or a Minimally Conscious State (MCS), she was not in imminent danger of death as long as she continued to receive food and water through the feeding tube. When the feeding tube was removed, at her husband's insistence, it took her thirteen days to die of dehydration, approximately the same amount of time it would take any non-critically ill person to die of thirst.

The late Pope John Paul II called this creeping callousness of hearts "the culture of death." Our convenience-driven culture has created a specific language of "mercy killing," which is supposed to act in defense of the poor victims who should have "the right to die" and "death with dignity."

My son, if sinners entice you, do not consent. If they say, "Come with us, let us lie in wait to shed blood; let us lurk secretly for the innocent without cause"; my son, do not walk in the way with them, Keep your foot from their path; for their feet run to evil, and they make haste to shed blood.
—Proverbs 1:10–11, 15–16

Look at the Lord's warning in Proverbs 1 to those who speak with reasoning but stand against God's truth:

✦ Watch out for enticing offers to be popular or to fit in (v. 10).

✦ Don't consent to anything that must be done "in secret" (v. 11).

✦ Don't hang out with the wrong crowd (v. 15).

✦ Don't be misled by evil disguised as reasoning (v. 16).

infuse (in FYOOZ) : to cause to be permeated with something (as a principle or quality) that alters usually for the better

How Did Our Society Get to Such Debased Thinking in Ethics?

There are several reasons:

1. Man's sinfulness

There are many factors that led to this atrocious thinking, but its source began with the first murderer, Cain. Genesis 4:8–10 tells the story: "And it came to pass, when they were in the field, that Cain rose up against Abel his brother and killed him. Then the LORD said to Cain, 'Where is Abel your brother?' He said, 'I do not know. Am I my brother's keeper?' And He said, 'What have you done? The voice of your brother's blood cries out to Me from the ground.'"

Cain decided that his brother's life was disposable. So he killed him, buried him, and went about his business.

Knowing that Cain had murdered his brother, God gave him a chance to take responsibility for his sin. He asked Cain, "Where is your brother?" In response, Cain coldly lied: "I do not know."

2. The Supreme Court's 1973 *Roe v. Wade* decision to legalize abortion

This decision has brutalized society's understanding of the unique value of each human life. A country cannot stand by while one of every three babies is aborted—and has been for more than three decades—without devaluing the societal attitude toward human life.

 Why do people choose the popular view over the scriptural, ethical standard?

✦ They don't know or understand the truth.

✦ They want to fit in.

✦ It's easier.

✦ Their hearts are far from God.

✦ Other: _____

3. The culture's increasing disregard for the truth of God's Word

For Christians, the moral compass for these ethical issues is God's clear revelation of Himself in Scripture:

✦ *God forbids murder.* "You shall not murder" (Exodus 20:13).

✦ *God hates murder of the innocent:* "These six things the LORD hates, yes, seven are an abomination to Him: a proud look, a lying tongue, hands that shed innocent blood . . ." (Proverbs 6:16–17).

✦ *God created all human beings in His image and gave them value.* "In the day that God created man, He made him in the likeness of God" (Genesis 5:1).

✦ *People who are infirmed, mentally challenged, and physically handicapped are created by God in His own image and are equally valuable to Him, and thus, must be to us.* "So the LORD said to him, 'Who has made man's mouth? Or who makes the mute, the deaf, the seeing, or the blind? Have not I, the LORD?'" (Exodus 4:11). "You shall not curse the deaf, nor put a stumbling block before the blind, but shall fear your God: I am the LORD" (Leviticus 19:14).

In what specific way can you go out of your way to be kind, care for, or do a favor for someone who is elderly, infirm, or mentally or physically disabled this week? Do you know someone already? Pray for an opportunity to minister to that person.

◆ *People are to show merciful care for the suffering and the weak.* "And the King will answer and say to them, 'Assuredly, I say to you, inasmuch as you did it to one of the least of these My brethren, you did it to Me'" (Matthew 25:40).

What is ONE THING you could do this week to minister to the "suffering and the weak"? Donate money, clothing, or your time? Invite someone to a meal? Volunteer at a ministry?

◆ *We are to accept God's will for both life and death.* In the Garden of Gethsemane, the Lord Jesus provided us with a supreme example of how Christians should approach death. Facing an intense spiritual and physical struggle concerning His coming death on the cross, Jesus prayed, "Father, if it is Your will, take this cup away from Me; nevertheless not My will, but Yours, be done" (Luke 22:42).

All of the "right to life" issues—abortion, cloning, euthanasia—are rooted in selfishness:

+ *Abortion*—focuses on the right of the *mother*, not the *child.* If having a baby is too hard or inconvenient for mom, then she chooses to kill the baby.

+ *Cloning*—kills as many embryos as necessary to get to the one that a person wants or needs.

+ *Euthanasia*—focuses on the convenience of society, not the rights of the elderly or handicapped. Why take care of a person you can destroy?

Contrast this to the deep, intense, unconditional love of God. He loves every life without regard to circumstance, need, ability, or handicap, and He sees potential in every new life.

+ *The idea that an individual has a "right to die" is totally at odds with the Christian belief that we are under God's authority.* "Or do you not know that your body is the temple of the Holy Spirit who is in you, whom you have from God, and you are not your own? For you were bought at a price; therefore glorify God in your body and in your spirit, which are God's" (1 Corinthians 6:19–20).

+ *Christians should not fear death.* The apostle Paul proclaimed that he was not afraid of death: "For me to live is Christ, and to die is gain" (Philippians 1:21). And he encourages all Christians not to be afraid of death: "We are confident, yes, well pleased rather to be absent from the body and to be present with the Lord" (2 Corinthians 5:8).

Whenever euthanasia issues are discussed, a critical distinction must be made between *active measures* that are taken to shorten life as opposed to *not taking extraordinary or heroic measures* to prolong life when death is imminent.

✦ Active measures to shorten life would be lethal injection, lethal medical overdose, or other more violent means of actively killing another human being.

✦ Not taking extraordinary measures to prolong the life of a terminally ill individual is a decision made by the patient or the family in consultation with their physician. They understand that death is imminent and they wish for no more extraordinary measures to be taken to prolong life.

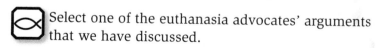

diffuse (di FYOOZ) : to pour out and permit or cause to spread freely; to extend, scatter

Select one of the euthanasia advocates' arguments that we have discussed.

Now choose a Scripture above that defeats that opinion.

📖 Do you know anyone who is unsure of what to believe about "right to life" issues? Write his or her name on the following lines, and begin this week to pray for that person:

What particular Scripture(s) would you be able to share with him or her?

As Dr. C. Everett Koop, former U. S. Surgeon General, put it:

"We must be wary of those who are too willing to end the lives of the elderly and the ill. If we ever decide that a poor quality of life justifies ending that life, we have taken a step down a slippery slope that places all of us in danger. There is a difference between allowing nature to take its course and actively assisting death. The call for euthanasia surfaces in our society periodically, as it is doing now under the guise of 'death with dignity' or assisted suicide. Euthanasia is a concept . . . that is in direct conflict with a religious and ethical tradition in which

The Terri Schiavo case was euthanasia, pure and simple. As a consequence of the judicial conclusions in the case, all physically ill Americans who are mentally challenged and those who are terminally ill are less safe from having their lives actively shortened than before.

the human race is presented with 'a blessing and a curse, life and death' and we are instructed 'therefore, to choose life.' I believe euthanasia lies outside the commonly held life-centered values of the West and cannot be allowed without incurring great social and personal tragedy. This is not merely an intellectual conundrum. This issue in-values actual human beings at risk."[6]

 Many of the issues in this study guide are emotion-ally-charged, and it can be difficult to see reason and truth in the wake of emotions and tears. The Christian leader is confident of the truth of God's Word but is careful to balance love and truth. Ask God to touch your heart with deep compassion for those you will meet who need to be strengthened to do the right thing.

FUSE BOX

We must reassert the sanctity-of-life ethic to protect all human beings.

PRIVATE WORLD DEVOTIONS

MONDAY: See it. Read the surrounding passages or chapter for the Key Scripture so that you can get an understanding of the background and context. This helps you to really *see* the verse.

TUESDAY: Hear it. Read the daily Key Scripture and/or surrounding passage out loud, putting your name in, if applicable. For example, <u>John</u> *can do all things through Christ. Thieves have come to destroy* <u>John</u>, *but Jesus has come that* <u>John</u> *might have eternal life.*

WEDNESDAY: Write it. Write the verse and then what it says about:

- ✦ *Others:* Respond, serve, and love as Jesus would.
- ✦ *Me:* Specific attitudes, choices, or habits.
- ✦ *God:* His love, mercy, holiness, peace, joy, etc.

PRIVATE WORLD JOURNAL

I am grateful for—I praise You for—I am
feeling—I am thinking—I need help with

PRIVATE WORLD DEVOTIONS *(Continued)*

THURSDAY: Memorize it. Take the verse with you—write it on a card or put it in your phone, iPod, or PDA. Go over it throughout the day so that it begins to *live* in your heart and mind.

FRIDAY: Pray it. Personalize the verse as you pray for yourself or for others or in praise to God. To pray is literally "to think about." Try thinking out loud or writing in your **PRIVATE WORLD JOURNAL.**

SATURDAY: Share it. Ask the Lord to bring someone to mind or in your path today who needs good news. Don't be shy—just let it out! Whether you IM, write, text, tell, or send it, the joy of God's Word will flow from your heart into theirs.

PRAYER REQUESTS

Date	Name	Need	Answer

PRIVATE WORLD JOURNAL

I am grateful for—I praise You for—I am feeling—I am thinking—I need help with

NOTES

CHAPTER 3

GENETIC ENGINEERING AND CLONING
WOULD YOU LIKE GREEN OR BLUE EYES WITH THAT?

KEY SCRIPTURE

I will praise You, for I am fearfully and wonderfully made; marvelous are Your works, and that my soul knows very well. My frame was not hidden from You, when I was made in secret, and skillfully wrought in the lowest parts of the earth. Your eyes saw my substance, being yet unformed. And in Your book they all were written, the days fashioned for me, when as yet there were none of them.
—Psalm 139:14–16

IN THE NEWS

Molly Nash was born with a rare blood disorder called Fanconi's anemia. She needed a bone marrow transplant for long-term survival, so her parents chose to produce another child using Preimplantation Genetic Diagnosis, or PGD. In doing so, they could not only avoid having a child with the same fatal genetic blood disorder, but they could also select embryos who would be a tissue match for Molly's bone marrow transplant. After much planning, Molly received her little brother Adam's umbilical blood and was success-fully treated and cured.[1]

This sounds like a happy ending, and it was for Molly. But this story has to be judged by the absolute truth of God's Word, not on emotion.

The Nashes genetically engineered thirty embryos—that is, thir-ty human beings—through test-tube fertilization. Using PGD, they found that only five babies had the right genetic code. On the fourth attempt at implantation, success was achieved. So nearly thirty ba-bies were created and killed for the purpose of having a child who met the parents' requirements. This is immoral and unethical even for the noble reason of treating an ill child. It must be remembered that Molly and Adam were no more precious in God's sight than the nearly thirty other babies who were discarded and destroyed.

IT'S TRUE!

✦ 87% of Americans believe that cloning a human is morally wrong.[2]

✦ 77% of teens believe that genetic engineering will have "some" to "a lot" of influence on their future.[3]

transfuse (trans FYOOZ) : to cause to pass from one to another; transmit

It wasn't that long ago that a reference to cloning peo-ple was only used in science fiction movies, and genetic engineering was a remote idea of the future. The sepa-rate but related issues of cloning and genetic engineer-ing highlight the amazing scientific and technological advances that have been made in the last decade. The future is here.

Scientists now understand the basic building blocks of life at the earliest stages of human development. Con-sequently, we have the power to create and manipulate human fetal development as never before in history. This forces us to face new and complex ethical decisions no humans before us have confronted.

I will praise You, for I am fearfully and wonderfully made; marvelous are Your works, and that my soul knows very well. My frame was not hidden from You, when I was made in secret, and skillfully wrought in the lowest parts of the earth. Your eyes saw my substance, being yet unformed. And in Your book they all were written, the days fashioned for me, when as yet there were none of them. —**Psalm 139:14–16**

We know from Scripture that the moment the human sperm and egg unite, a unique genetic individual is created. He or she . . .

✦ has the right to life by virtue of being a human being, healthy or not, normal or not, wanted or not;

✦ is of incalculable value to God, from conception onward (even test-tube conception);

✦ has a life that is sacred (is created in God's image).

No human being has the right to decide to devalue or discard life for any reason.

infuse (in FYOOZ) ; to cause to be permeated with something (as a principle or quality) that alters usually for the better

CLONING

What is *cloning*?

✦ Cloning is a process of reproducing an offspring, animal or human, with genetic material from only one adult, rather than half the material from each parent.

How are clones made?

✦ A clone is made by emptying all of the genetic material from a mother's egg and then inserting material from an adult's cell into the egg. Then an electric spark is applied that stimulates the egg to begin the division process.[4]

✦ After a period of four to five days of cell division and growth, the cloned egg-embryo can be used in two ways:

1. It can be implanted in the uterus of a prospective mother-to-be, where it will continue to grow and develop in utero until birth. This is called *reproductive cloning*.

2. It can be used in *therapeutic cloning*—that is, the extraction of stem cells from cloned human embryos for the purpose of finding cures for the diseases of older and bigger human beings. In the process, the human embryo's life is destroyed.

Conception Versus Cloning

When a woman's egg is fertilized by a man's sperm, it is called *conception,* and the resulting child will have attributes and genetic material from both mother and father.

In the *cloning* process, the newborn clone baby will be the virtual genetic identical twin of the adult cell donor only. The only real difference between the clone and the donor is the chronological age difference between the adult cell donor and the newborn clone.

> [They] exchanged the truth of God for the lie, and worshiped and served the creature rather than the Creator, who is blessed forever. Amen.
> —Romans 1:25

There Are Huge Ethical Problems with the Process of Cloning

Cloning is an extremely dangerous process, with most clones dying or being destroyed before maturation because of horrendous and often fatal development abnormalities.

You may be familiar with the case of the sheep named Dolly, the first successful higher mammal clone. The process to create her took 277 attempts, out of which came 29 growing embryos and only one pregnancy and live birth, Dolly.

Dolly has now been put to sleep after developing arthritis and a progressive lung disease. These diseases of old age are not commonly found in sheep in the prime of life, like Dolly was.

It appears that clones may have two age factors:

1. Their reproductive age is not consistent with their chronological age.

2. The age of their cells and organs is closer to the age of their adult cell donor.

This results in a dilemma: Suppose a thirty-year-old mother produced a clone daughter of herself. Fifteen years later, she is forty-five and the clone daughter is fifteen, chronologically. Because the clone's cell and organ age is now about forty-five, would the fifteen-year-old be experiencing puberty or menopause at that time?

Reproductive Cloning Carries Immoral and Dangerous Risks

✦ Reproductive cloning greatly raises the risk that horrifically deformed clone babies with agonizingly painful and debilitating birth defects will soon emerge from cloning clinics.

✦ Reproductive cloning raises the real possibility of the adult cell donors claiming that the clones are their property rather than their children, thus denying the legal and moral protectors of personhood to the newborn clone:

◈ The newborn could be sold or traded by the donor.

◈ In the case of a divorce, would the clone be considered a child or property?

✦ Reproductive cloning could eventually lead to the exploitation of women:

◈ Their eggs could become a commodity in the marketplace.

◈ Women could be encouraged to take the potentially harmful hormone treatments required for the retrieval of their eggs.

Therapeutic Cloning Is Morally Reprehensible and Should Be Opposed by Christians

Although therapeutic or research cloning sounds beneficial, it is immoral because the embryo must be destroyed in the process.

The harvesting of embryonic stem cells for research also carries the same potential to become a vast business of cloning to kill for profit. Women would be paid for their eggs to use in the mass production of human clone embryos for the express purpose of "dismembering for research."

✦ In therapeutic cloning, human beings consciously choose to create a human embryo for the express purpose of killing it.

Cloning Has No Foundation in Scripture
No matter how much science advances . . .

✦ *Science will never be able to create out of nothing as God did.* "And the LORD God formed man of the dust of the ground, and breathed into his nostrils the breath of life; and man became a living being" (Genesis 2:7).

✦ *Science will never be able to create out of love.* "We love Him because He first loved us" (1 John 4:19).

✦ *Science will never be intimately involved with the life of a child.* "My frame was not hidden from You, when I was made in secret, and skillfully wrought in the lowest parts of the earth. Your eyes saw my substance, being yet unformed. And in Your book they all were written, the days fashioned for me, when as yet there were none of them" (Psalm 139:15–16).

GROUP DISCUSSION

Contrast the logic of science and cloning with creation and the intense love of God. Note that there are different motives at the start and different motives for the lifetime.

49

Scripture Reveals God's Involvement in the Conception and Birth of Children

 The Bible tells us that children are given by the Lord as treasured gifts.

✦ *Eve proclaimed that she received her child from the Lord Himself.* "Adam knew Eve his wife, and she conceived and bore Cain, and said, 'I have acquired a man from the LORD' (Genesis 4:1).

✦ *Jacob gratefully acknowledged that his children were a gift from the Lord.* "He lifted his eyes and saw the women and children, and said, 'Who are these with you?' So he said, 'The children whom God has graciously given your servant'" (Genesis 33:5).

✦ *Isaiah believed that his children were miraculously given to him by God.* "Here am I and the children whom the LORD has given me! We are for signs and wonders in Israel from the LORD of hosts, Who dwells in Mount Zion" (Isaiah 8:18).

diffuse (di FYOOZ) ; to pour out and permit or cause to spread freely; to extend, scatter

STEM-CELL RESEARCH

Certain celebrities have chosen to use the issue of stem-cell research to make Christians look unreasonable. The truth is that Christians' enthusiasm about the prospect of adult stem-cell research and its resulting therapies to bring amazing relief to millions of suffering people is genuine. However, we reject the immoral practice of *embryonic* stem-cell research.

It's easy to line up on the popular side of celebrities and the media. As a student leader, you need to know your stuff and take the lead to help others understand it also.

Most people do not understand the distinctions between *embryonic* stem cells and *adult* stem cells when they talk about this issue.

- *Embryonic stem cells* can only be obtained by destroying a human life.

- *Adult stem cells* can be obtained from a person without causing harm. From the umbilical cord blood after a baby is born to a person's nasal passages, there are myriad places to obtain stem cells in the human body that will not require the death of the person.[5]

GENETIC ENGINEERING

As a result of the massively federally funded project known as the Human Genome Project (HGP), we have now mapped the sequence of the three billion base pairs of DNA that together complete the human genetic blueprint, known as a "genome." In simple terms, this means we know which genes control:

- Hair color, eye color, skin pigmentation, height, allergies, intelligence, and athletic aptitude;

- Conditions such as Alzheimer's disease, cancer, cystic fibrosis, diabetes, Down syndrome, muscular dystrophy, and other diseases.

The advancements of science can be presented as positive when you disregard the humanity of the embryo. Be ready to present *truth over logic*.

Although Science Holds Great Promise, It Also Introduces Great Danger

The selfishness of our culture has increased in acceptance of a quality-of-life ethic as opposed to a sanctity-of-life ethic.

✦ This cultivates a dangerous practice of "playing God" by choosing to keep healthy embryos but to kill embryos—human babies—who are less than perfect, such as the handicapped or impaired.

✦ Our ability to identify and diagnose ailments continues to exceed our ability to treat them. With genetic mapping, parents are being advised to terminate the pregnancy through abortion and "try again" if a potential birth defect is discovered.

✦ For PGD, a woman is given drugs to cause her to hyperovulate or create a large number of eggs. The eggs are then harvested and fertilized in vitro in test tubes and tested for certain genetic markers. The embryos with the genetic markers for disease are destroyed and those deemed healthy are transferred to the mother's uterus for reproduction.

Such procedures, and the thinking that goes with them:

✦ lead directly to creating and discarding human embryos deemed less desirable;

✦ create a mind-set that justifies the process of human selection.

In all that you have learned in this lesson, what is ONE THING about cloning, stem-cell research, or genetic engineering that you could focus on learning so well that you would be able to speak or write about it if asked?

FUSE BOX

Both reproductive and therapeutic cloning, if embraced by society, will lead America rapidly to a dark and dangerous place. As Christians, we need to oppose these practices and embrace the truth of God's Word.

PRIVATE WORLD DEVOTIONS

MONDAY: See it. Read the surrounding passages or chapter for the Key Scripture so that you can get an understanding of the background and context. This helps you to really *see* the verse.

TUESDAY: Hear it. Read the daily Key Scripture and/or surrounding passage out loud, putting your name in, if applicable. For example, <u>John</u> *can do all things through Christ. Thieves have come to destroy* <u>John</u>, *but Jesus has come that* <u>John</u> *might have eternal life.*

WEDNESDAY: Write it. Write the verse and then what it says about:

- ✦ *Others:* Respond, serve, and love as Jesus would.
- ✦ *Me:* Specific attitudes, choices, or habits.
- ✦ *God:* His love, mercy, holiness, peace, joy, etc.

PRIVATE WORLD JOURNAL

I am grateful for—I praise You for—I am feeling—I am thinking—I need help with

PRIVATE WORLD DEVOTIONS *(Continued)*

THURSDAY: Memorize it. Take the verse with you—write it on a card or put it in your phone, iPod, or PDA. Go over it throughout the day so that it begins to *live* in your heart and mind.

FRIDAY: Pray it. Personalize the verse as you pray for yourself or for others or in praise to God. To pray is literally "to think about." Try thinking out loud or writing in your **PRIVATE WORLD JOURNAL.**

SATURDAY: Share it. Ask the Lord to bring someone to mind or in your path today who needs good news. Don't be shy—just let it out! Whether you IM, write, text, tell, or send it, the joy of God's Word will flow from your heart into theirs.

PRAYER REQUESTS

Date	Name	Need	Answer

PRIVATE WORLD JOURNAL

I am grateful for—I praise You for—I am feeling—I am thinking—I need help with

NOTES

CHAPTER 4

PORNOGRAPHY:
IT'S JUST ONE LOOK, RIGHT?

KEY SCRIPTURE

For all that is in the world—the lust of the flesh,
the lust of the eyes, and the pride of life—is
not of the Father but is of the world.

—1 John 2:16

COULD THIS BE YOU?

He didn't mean to look. Matt was surfing the Internet for his ninth-grade history project, and there it was—porn. One wrong click and he was looking at X-rated photos of nude people in sexual positions. At first he was embarrassed and quickly clicked out of the site, but he couldn't shake those images from his mind. Later that night, after everyone was asleep, he went back to look again.

> **God created sex:**
>
> ✦ to be holy, not dirty;
>
> ✦ to be private and intimate, not flaunted and publicly discussed.

What started as an honest mistake soon turned into an obsession. Matt was curious about sex, and there were more than enough Web sites, chat rooms, and blogs to feed his curiosity. He became bolder in his viewing and started spending more and more time on the computer searching for something even more extreme.

Matt's new hobby started affecting his life at school. He started looking at the girls and teachers differently, undressing them in his mind. He couldn't concentrate on schoolwork, lost interest in sports, and didn't spend as much time with friends. Internet porn quickly became an addiction.

IT'S TRUE!

✦ 90% of 8- to 16-year-olds with Internet access have viewed porn online (mostly while doing homework). The average age of first exposure to Internet pornography is 11 years old, with the largest consumers of Internet pornography being 12- to 17-year-olds. 47% of computer users who visit explicit Web sites are 12 to 18-year-old females.[1]

✦ 75% of prime-time television shows include sexual content. 23% of couples depicted on television as having intercourse appear to be or play characters ages 18-24. 10% of shows on television include sexual content involving teenagers.[2]

✦ Playboy TV is available in 24 million of the nation's 81 million homes that receive either satellite cable or digital television.[3]

✦ 3 out of 4 teens say one reason teenagers have sex is that "TV shows and movies make it seem normal for teenagers to have sex."[4]

✦ 13- to 15-year-olds rank entertainment media as the top source of information about sexuality and sexual health.[5]

✦ Studies show there is a causal link between violent pornography and aggressive behavior toward women. Exposure to sexually explicit material that is not violent, but nevertheless degrades women, bears "some causal relationship to the level of sexual violence."[6]

✦ The only explicit, hard-core sexual material that is absolutely illegal in the U.S. today is child pornography.[7]

transfuse (trans FYOOZ) : to cause to pass from one to another; transmit

God designed humans, and He created sexual expression. Satan has attempted to counterfeit genuine human sexuality with a malignancy called pornography.

This corruption is a direct rebellion against God's divine plan for human sexuality. You may know people who say pornography is a harmless pastime, one that involves just the looker and doesn't harm anyone else, but those are lies.

To really understand this cheap counterfeit, we must first understand the majesty and beauty of God's original design for human sexual expression.

And the Lord God said, "It is not good that man should be alone; I will make him a helper comparable to him." —**Genesis 2:18**

Therefore a man shall leave his father and mother and be joined to his wife, and they shall become one flesh. And they were both naked, the man and his wife, and were not ashamed. —**Genesis 2:24–25**

God's plan for human sexual expression is divine.

- ✦ God created human beings as male and female.

- ✦ Both genders "are of equal worth before God."

- ✦ Both males and females reveal differing facets of God's divine image.[8]

+ The divine "gift of gender . . . is part of the goodness of God's creation."[9]

+ Man and woman compliment each other.

+ God's divine design for human beings is that they become "one flesh" through the union of sexual intercourse.

God's original intention for sex is one man and one woman, joined in a divine design of sexual intimacy in marriage. Through this, the two are blessed, completed, and joined together as *one flesh* in a bond that cannot be duplicated. Through this intimacy, husband and wife will never be completely separated from one another again.

The culture's intention for sex is recreation and self-gratification and has little regard for a relationship. Is it any wonder that many women and men are emotionally scarred and keep looking for love in all the wrong places?

For all that is in the world—the lust of the flesh, the lust of the eyes, and the pride of life—is not of the Father but is of the world.

—1 John 2:16

When you consider God's plan for sexuality, how does this affect you as you think about dating and relationships? What type of person are you looking for?

_____

_____

_____

Jesus, responding to hostile questioning from Pharisees, emphatically reaffirms God's original design for marriage and human sexual expression. "'For this reason a man shall leave his father and mother and be joined to his wife, and the two shall become one flesh'? So then, they are no longer two but one flesh. Therefore what God has joined together, let not man separate" (Matthew 19:5–6).

Pornography Has Taken God's Holy Sexual Design and Made It Impure

Those who make pornography have taken the most giving, loving, and intimate human relation God has given us—sexual intercourse—and transformed it into something impure, ugly, perverted, and destructive. In our culture today, vile and gutter terms for the act of sex have become synonymous for acts of extreme hostility, exploitation, and aggression.

Pornography Is Rooted in Selfishness and Self-Gratification

The existence of pornography as a satanic counterfeit of sex is powerful evidence that we live in a fallen world wracked by spiritual warfare.

Pornography:

- ✦ perverts and distorts all of the God-given purposes for sexual intimacy;

- ✦ feeds "the lust of the flesh, and the lust of the eyes, and the pride of life" and encourages self-gratification (1 John 2:16).

That Christ may dwell in your hearts through faith; that you, being rooted and grounded in love may be able to comprehend with all the saints what is the width and length and depth and height—to know the love of Christ which passes knowledge; that you may be filled with all the fullness of God. —**Ephesians 3:17–19**

The love of Christ. The fullness of God. These words cannot coexist with pornography.

Define *love* and *lust* by using the following words: *self, unconditional, caring, self-control, others, preoccupied, focused, out of control, pure, perverts, destroys, encourages, uplifts.*

Love: _____

_____

Lust: _____

_____

God's Plan Is for a Husband and Wife to Become One Flesh

God designed marriage to be a mutually satisfying, caring, intimate relationship. The sexual act is only part of a life together. It is never about self-gratification.

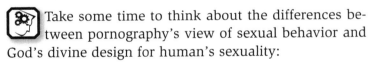 Take some time to think about the differences between pornography's view of sexual behavior and God's divine design for human's sexuality:

Pornography	**God's Design**
presents human beings as mere objects of desire, to be used and discarded;	teaches that a relationship between a man and woman is based on love and respect;
encourages men and women to have sex with multiple partners;	makes two people into one flesh;
shows sexual intercourse as merely a casual, recreational, and superficial form of self-gratification.	exalts sexual intimacy as mutually satisfying and caring.

diffuse (di FYOOZ); to pour out and permit or cause to spread freely; to extend, scatter

Why Is Pornography Destructive?

✦ *Because sex is powerful.* God created sex as an essential part of our humanity. Sex's power to destroy, as distorted by pornography, is like a nuclear bomb. It can, and has, destroyed lives and leveled marriages just as nuclear bombs have killed people and destroyed cities.

Lust—usually intense or unbridled sexual desire: LASCIVIOUSNESS.

An intense longing: CRAVING.

✦ *Because pornography is addictive.* This addictive process of pornography is well documented both in terms of process and result.[10] The pornographic material available on the Internet and through magazines, videos, and DVDs is vile and destitute to the extreme and is getting more depraved with each passing month.

Those who continually expose themselves to this spiritual and emotional toxic waste can become addicted, and having become addicted, will escalate to ever more hard-core material in order to get the same emotional "buzz" they have come to expect. Subject matter that in the past would have shocked them is now welcomed as they become increasingly desensitized to the ever more hard-core images and material they seek. Some who have become addicted will adopt deviant and violent sexual lifestyles as they act upon their pornography-fed fantasies.

◆ 87% of sexual molesters of girls and 77% of sexual molesters of boys were frequent users of hard-core pornography.[11]

GROUP DISCUSSION

Hard-core pornography is violent and degrades women. But what about "soft-core" pornography, such as what is seen in R-rated movies, late-night HBO, and some magazines? Is that OK? Why or why not?

_____

_____

_____

Suppose tomorrow someone pulls you aside with an invitation to watch a questionable movie. It might not be porn, but it is R–rated for sexual content.

What do you say?

_____

_____

_____

What are your reasons for watching or not watching the movie? List three:

1. _____

2. _____

3. _____

It is as spiritually and emotionally foolish to expose one-self to pornography as it would be physically foolish to expose oneself to radioactive material.

GROUP DISCUSSION

Pornography on the Internet is not illegal. Does that mean it is not immoral?

Have friends or acquaintances talked to you about pornography?

How does this make you feel?

Establish Pure Thought Patterns to Banish the Grip of Pornography

If pornography continues to be rampant in the culture, how can a Christian leader protect his or her heart?

The Lord will never leave you powerless in any situation. He has left instructions throughout the Word of

God for every dilemma. In the case of pornography, you might not be able to stop the images from pouring in through the TV, movies, or Internet, but you can fill your mind and heart with so many pure and good thoughts that these destructive images will be overtaken and forced out. You can, and you must.

> *Finally, brethren, whatever things are true, whatever things are noble, whatever things are just, whatever things are pure, whatever things are lovely, whatever things are of good report, if there is any virtue and if there is anything praiseworthy—meditate on these things.* **—Philippians 4:8**

+ *whatever things are true.* The truth of God's Word concerning human sexuality, which will never let you down, not the "feel-good" lie of the culture, which promises satisfaction but cannot perform it.[12]

+ *whatever things are noble.* This is the same as *honorable* or "that which has the dignity of holiness on it."[13] The seriousness of this definition makes it easy for you to discern if a thought or action is *noble*.

+ *whatever things are just.* The Christian chooses responsibility over pleasure, serving God over satisfying self.

+ *whatever things are pure.* Pure thoughts are morally undefiled thoughts. In the day of Paul's writing, the Greek word *hagnos* was used ceremonially to describe something that has been cleansed so it is fit to be brought into the presence of God and used in His service. Focus your thoughts on what you can present to God in thought and prayer.

✦ *whatever things are lovely.* This is an interesting word picture that describes something so lovely that you are drawn to it, attracted to it. The Greek word is *prosphiles,* and it might be paraphrased as "that which calls forth love."[14]

> Lust is a selfish desire for self-gratification that is preoccupied with self to the exclusion of God and other human beings.

✦ *whatever things are of good report.* These are the inner thoughts that work toward forming your outward reputation, thoughts that you would be happy to speak about and not be ashamed.

✦ *if there is any virtue.* Virtue speaks of excellence, and Paul is careful to note that if there is *any virtue* in any part of life, we should think about it.

   ✦ In your studies, let excellence be your goal.

   ✦ In relationships, strive for excellence.

   ✦ In your daily thought life, settle for nothing less than excellence.

This leaves no room for "degrees" of sexual thought and allows nothing less than a whole person dedicated to a life of virtue and excellence in all things.

✦ *if there is anything praiseworthy.* There is so much to think about that is worthy of praise—God's character of forgiveness, mercy, holiness, and His deep abiding love for you.

When you set a habit of focusing your mind on what is *true, noble, just, pure, lovely, of good report, virtuous,* and *praiseworthy*, then you crowd out evil thoughts. You are drawn to the plan of God for your life and repelled by temptation to go against it.

What is ONE THING you can choose to meditate on this week that is found in Philippians 4:8? Circle the word to focus on:

noble

true

just

pure

lovely

of good report

virtuous

praiseworthy

Write down the thought based on this word:

_____

_____

_____

You are aware of the readily available stream of porn that your friends face every day through media, Internet, and peers. What is ONE THING about the truth of divine sexuality or the character of God that you can share with others this week that might help them to walk away from the destruction of pornography?

_____

_____

_____

[FUSE BOX]

A focused thought life takes the power out of pornography, and that is the place you want to be.

_____

_____

_____

_____

_____

_____

_____

_____

_____

_____

_____

PRIVATE WORLD DEVOTIONS

MONDAY: See it. Read the surrounding passages or chapter for the Key Scripture so that you can get an understanding of the background and context. This helps you to really *see* the verse.

TUESDAY: Hear it. Read the daily Key Scripture and/or surrounding passage out loud, putting your name in, if applicable. For example, <u>John</u> *can do all things through Christ. Thieves have come to destroy* <u>John</u>, *but Jesus has come that* <u>John</u> *might have eternal life.*

WEDNESDAY: Write it. Write the verse and then what it says about:

✦ *Others:* Respond, serve, and love as Jesus would.

✦ *Me:* Specific attitudes, choices, or habits.

✦ *God:* His love, mercy, holiness, peace, joy, etc.

PRIVATE WORLD JOURNAL

I am grateful for—I praise You for—I am feeling—I am thinking—I need help with

PRIVATE WORLD DEVOTIONS *(Continued)*

THURSDAY: Memorize it. Take the verse with you—write it on a card or put it in your phone, iPod, or PDA. Go over it throughout the day so that it begins to *live* in your heart and mind.

FRIDAY: Pray it. Personalize the verse as you pray for yourself or for others or in praise to God. To pray is literally "to think about." Try thinking out loud or writing in your **PRIVATE WORLD JOURNAL.**

SATURDAY: Share it. Ask the Lord to bring someone to mind or in your path today who needs good news. Don't be shy—just let it out! Whether you IM, write, text, tell, or send it, the joy of God's Word will flow from your heart into theirs.

PRAYER REQUESTS

Date	Name	Need	Answer

PRIVATE WORLD JOURNAL

I am grateful for—I praise You for—I am feeling—I am thinking—I need help with

NOTES

CHAPTER 5

TEEN SEX and TECHNICAL VIRGINITY:
HOW FAR IS TOO FAR?

Note: This lesson should be taught in gender-specific classrooms.

KEY SCRIPTURE

"You have heard that it was said, 'You shall not commit adultery.' But I tell you, everyone who looks at a woman to lust for her has already committed adultery with her in his heart"

—Matthew 5:27–28

COULD THIS BE YOU?

Laura and Tommy were childhood sweethearts, raised in the church, and active in the youth group. One night on a date, temptation took over and they both gave in to a make-out session gone too far. They had dated for three years and had tried to be so good! At first, they both cried in shame and waited in fear of pregnancy. Two months went by with no sign of pregnancy, and they both breathed a sigh of relief. But now that they had experienced sexual intimacy, it seemed that they were tempted more often, and it became harder and harder to say "no."

> If it involves a sex organ, then it is sex.
> —Dr. Phil McGraw

Within the year, Laura became pregnant and three lives were altered forever. "I never thought it would happen to us," Tommy later told his youth group. "But it did. And we learned that giving in one time is one time too many."

IT'S TRUE!

Teenagers in America today face an unprecedented situation.

✦ In 1970, the average first-time marriage ages were: men, 23.2 years old; women, 20.8 years old. In 1998, the average first-time marriage ages were: men, 25.0 years old; women, 26.7 years old.[1]

✦ Society expects young adults to wait longer for marriage, but that same society is saturated with sexuality and sexualized messages in pop-culture entertainment and commercial advertising.

✦ In previous generations, it would have been possible to go through an entire day without hearing a sexualized or sexually suggestive comment, but no longer. In early twenty-first-century America, exposure to sexual comments and situations are almost constant.

✦ During the 1999–2000 television season, 68% of all shows contained some sexual content.[2] This sends a footnoted message: "This is normal."

THINK ABOUT IT

Think about the shows you watch on TV. Are there sexual commentary and situations in these shows?

Have they become so much the "norm" that you hardly notice them any more?

_____

_____

_____

How many times a day do you hear or see a sexual comment?

_____ at school

_____ in a magazine

_____ on the Internet (including IMs and chats)

_____ in a song

_____ from a friend

_____ on TV

_____ in a movie?

transfuse (trans FYOOZ); to cause to pass from one to another; transmit

This commonality of sexual messages and vaguely defined sexual boundaries has helped to bring about a new type of sex—that is, sexual experimentation. Students are now familiar with the term *technical virgin*, a false badge of honor that has become the new standard. Their only criterion for "virginity" is avoiding full-fledged sexual intercourse.

Many students have redefined sex to only include intercourse. They say that all other manner of sexual expression, such as mutual genital stimulation to orgasm or oral sex, are OK because those activities aren't really "sex."

Being a "technical virgin" has become an acceptable alternative for many teenagers.

Then God said, "Let Us make man in Our image, according to Our likeness; let them have dominion over the fish of the sea, over the birds of the air, and over the cattle, over all the earth and over every creeping thing that creeps on the earth." So God created man in His own image; in the image of God He created him; male and female He created them. **—Genesis 1:26–27**

Therefore a man shall leave his father and mother and be joined to his wife, and they shall become one flesh. And they were both naked, the man and his wife, and were not ashamed. **—Genesis 2:24–25**

Contemporary attitudes about sex are wrong from beginning to end. Sex is not a matter of technical definition. God created human beings as sexual beings, and His design for human sexuality is one man and one woman in a lifelong committed relationship called marriage.

infuse (in FYOOZ) : to cause to be permeated with something (as a principle or quality) that alters usually for the better

Which of these is true? Sex is:

_____ thrilling emotions and tingling sensations.

_____ sexual arousal and intercourse.

_____ sexual organs and reproductive systems.

_____ all of the above.

These definitions are all accurate, but very incomplete. They do not tell the story of the full dimension of the powerful purpose of sex as designed by the Creator.

✦ Sex is a basic, integral part of who God created us to be.

✦ Sex is everything about us that relates to being a male or a female human being created in God's image.

✦ Sex was created to be expressed and enjoyed in the marriage bed.

Sex was not a casual thought of God; it was divinely planned to be powerful and, therefore, has its own set of rules. God's intention was for us to protect this powerful human experience, one powerful enough to destroy lives and families if not properly channeled in its expression.

✦ *God created us as sexual beings.* "So God created man in His own image; in the image of God He created him; male and female He created them" (Genesis 1:27).

✦ *God included our sexuality when He pronounced His creation as "very good."* "God saw everything that He had made, and, behold, it was very good" (Genesis 1:31).

Many Christian counselors and ministers will tell you of counseling "technical virgins," male and female, who cannot delete non-intercourse, sexually related experiences and memories from their emotional "hard drives," as much as they try. As they prepare for marriage to the one to whom they want to give their whole sexual selves, they are fully aware that they have already given some of themselves away. This makes it difficult, if not impossible, to give all of themselves to a spouse.

✦ *Sex is blessed of God.* After Adam and Eve had fulfilled God's plan by becoming "one flesh," "they were both naked . . . and were not ashamed" (Genesis 2:24–25).

Alas, all that changed when sin entered the world. Nothing was the same, including sex.

While still a part of God's good creation, man's sin changed the sexual act:

✦ From "not ashamed" to potential sexual gratification without rules.

✦ From marital joy to potential destruction of families.

God's design for sex inside of marriage is clear in the Scriptures. He intends for one man and one woman to find completion in each other through physical intimacy as they experience:

✦ unity (Genesis 2:24–25),

✦ intimate knowledge (Genesis 4:1),

✦ procreation (Genesis 1:28),

✦ delight and joy (Proverbs 5:19),

✦ relaxation and satisfaction (Song of Solomon 2:8–17; 4:1–16),

✦ avoidance of sexual temptation. (1 Corinthians 7:2–5).

Sexual experimentation may seem harmless, and it may be viewed as normal by the culture, but that doesn't make it right.

TRUTH: All of God's good plan for the expression of our sexuality in positive, productive, nurturing ways within marriage is threatened, diminished, and endangered by premarital sexual experimentation and experience.

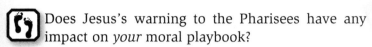 Ask yourself, "Am I content to live by a mere technicality?" Now really think about this. We know what God says, so do we try to mix in what the culture says, add an opinion, and come up with self-rule in sexual matters? What kind of life is that?

Christians who use this kind of fuzzy math to come up with their own sexual rules distort the truth of God's Word for their own benefit.

This is what the Pharisees tried to do, and Jesus called them on it. He said, "You have heard that it was said, 'You shall not commit adultery.' But I tell you, everyone who looks at a woman to lust for her has already committed adultery with her in his heart" (Matthew 5:27–28).

Jesus warned the Pharisees that technicality didn't count. Although they hadn't physically committed the sex act, they did commit adultery in the heart. Jesus let them know that *physical adultery* and *adultery in the heart* were one and the same.

Does Jesus's warning to the Pharisees have any impact on *your* moral playbook?

✦ Sexual sin occurs in the heart before it is played out in the body.

✦ Lust of the mind and heart precede the selfish desire for self-gratification.

✦ Flirtation can quickly degenerate into lustful desire.

✦ A touch of the private areas can quickly spark lustful physical arousal.

In case you are thinking that this is stretching the point or that we are overreacting, how about if we let Jesus say it nice and plain for you? "For from within, out of the heart of men, proceed evil thoughts, adulteries, fornications, murders" (Mark 7:21). Jesus grouped murder right next to fornication! He is serious about this stuff.

What is *fornication* anyway? Isn't that just for married people? In both of these verses the word is the translation of the Greek word *porneia*, which includes *all* sexual immorality, including, but not limited to, *pre- or extramarital* sexual intercourse.

GROUP DISCUSSION

Do you think that students try more sexual experimenting than they used to? Is oral sex talked about often in your circles?

✦ In a new kind of "spin the bottle," students as young as twelve are experimenting with oral sex, lesbianism, homosexuality, and sexual gratification.[3]

✦ Oral sex isn't considered sex by most teens.[4]

Let's get honest:

+ Can you engage in physical intimacy such as sexual foreplay, mutual genital stimulation, or oral sex and not have lustful, sinful desires for your partner that are defined by Jesus as adultery in your heart?

+ How far is too far?

Lots of questions, but the Bible only gives one answer and not even a hint more. *Sex is blessed inside of marriage; it is sin outside of marriage.*

What if I choose to do my own thing? How bad is it? The consequences are far too high to take such chances. They include:

> Flee sexual immorality. Every sin that a man does is outside the body, but he who commits sexual immorality sins against his own body.
> —1 Corinthians 6:18

+ strained fellowship with God (sin always interferes with our fellowship with the Father);

+ problems in your future marriage relationship;

+ a damaged testimony;

+ losing the power to help others.

diffuse (di FYOOZ): to pour out and permit or cause to spread freely; to extend, scatter

God's Plan for Sexual Purity
God does have a plan; He always does.

1. Be prepared.
Our model for successful living is the Old Testament hero Joseph. When his master's wife offered him a "no-

strings-attached" sexual liaison, he quickly said what was already in his heart: "How then can I do this great wickedness, and sin against God?" (Genesis 39:9).

What is ONE VERSE you can memorize this week from the lesson that will stay in your heart as an instant answer in times of temptation? Write it:

_____

_____

_____

2. Run away from sexual or provocative situations.

She didn't want to take "no" for an answer, so she persisted. Joseph literally ran out of the house, not even stopping to gather up the garment she had grabbed as he was running away (Genesis 39:12).

Don't try to dance close to the fire, because you will get morally roasted. Testing the situation is not avoiding sexual sin; it's welcoming it. To put oneself in intimate situations with the opposite sex and to engage in inappropriate touching and physical familiarity is the opposite of fleeing temptation. To go there is to walk right into the snare of the sexual sin of the mind and heart, which Jesus so clearly condemns.

3. Cultivate the mind-set of God.

Finally, brethren, whatever things are true, whatever things are noble, whatever things are just, whatever things are pure, whatever things are lovely, whatever things are of good report, if there is any virtue and if there is anything praiseworthy—meditate on these things. **—Philippians 4:8**

In this age of sexual confusion, flee temptation and preserve yourself for that one God has chosen as your life's partner.

4. Remember, everyone *isn't* doing it.
More and more teens are making the right moral decisions concerning sex.

+ 42% of America's teens believe it is wrong to have sex before marriage, compared with just 30% in 1977.[5]

GROUP DISCUSSION

What is the biggest struggle you face concerning moral purity?

5. Don't go it alone.

Hang out with like-minded people. Don't listen to popular opinion or rationalization.

Jesus understands this struggle. "For He Himself has said, 'I will never leave you nor forsake you'" (Hebrews 13:5).

In a culture flooded with people faltering under permissive codes of sexual conduct, we must model and teach an understanding of sex as God's good gift to humankind.

FUSE BOX

God has only one standard for men, women, boys, and girls: sex should only be between a husband and wife within the confines of holy matrimony.

NOTES

PRIVATE WORLD DEVOTIONS

MONDAY: See it. Read the surrounding passages or chapter for the Key Scripture so that you can get an understanding of the background and context. This helps you to really *see* the verse.

TUESDAY: Hear it. Read the daily Key Scripture and/or surrounding passage out loud, putting your name in, if applicable. For example, <u>John</u> *can do all things through Christ. Thieves have come to destroy* <u>John</u>, *but Jesus has come that* <u>John</u> *might have eternal life.*

WEDNESDAY: Write it. Write the verse and then what it says about:

✦ *Others:* Respond, serve, and love as Jesus would.

✦ *Me:* Specific attitudes, choices, or habits.

✦ *God:* His love, mercy, holiness, peace, joy, etc.

PRIVATE WORLD JOURNAL

I am grateful for—I praise You for—I am feeling—I am thinking—I need help with

PRIVATE WORLD DEVOTIONS *(Continued)*

THURSDAY: Memorize it. Take the verse with you—write it on a card or put it in your phone, iPod, or PDA. Go over it throughout the day so that it begins to *live* in your heart and mind.

FRIDAY: Pray it. Personalize the verse as you pray for yourself or for others or in praise to God. To pray is literally "to think about." Try thinking out loud or writing in your **PRIVATE WORLD JOURNAL.**

SATURDAY: Share it. Ask the Lord to bring someone to mind or in your path today who needs good news. Don't be shy—just let it out! Whether you IM, write, text, tell, or send it, the joy of God's Word will flow from your heart into theirs.

PRAYER REQUESTS

Date	Name	Need	Answer

PRIVATE WORLD JOURNAL

I am grateful for—I praise You for—I am feeling—I am thinking—I need help with

NOTES

CHAPTER 6

TEEN HOMOSEXUALITY:
CREATION OR CHOICE?

KEY SCRIPTURE

No temptation has overtaken you except such as is common to man; but God is faithful, who will not allow you to be tempted beyond what you are able, but with the temptation will also make the way of escape, that you may be able to bear it.
—1 Corinthians 10:13

COULD THIS BE YOU?

Joe didn't feel like he fit in with other boys but he craved attention from them to replace the attention he didn't get from his father. Early on, Joe began to sexualize his desire to be close to males, which only led to further confusion in his life. At 16, Joe started drinking at a party one night and had his first homosexual experience. By age 18, Joe was making his own decisions, dating older men, and going out to gay bars frequently.

Marilu felt uncomfortable around boys. When she confided this to her Christian friends, they proclaimed her as "weird." "Maybe you're gay," they laughed. She said, "no way," but the thought of it haunted her. Marilu stayed away from her

> Some think homosexuality is a modern movement, but it is a sexual sin that has been around for thousands of years.

friends and started to feel very alone. When she saw a Gay, Lesbian, Straight Education Network (GLSEN) ad at school, she decided to quietly investigate it. There she met gay teens who convinced her she should at least "try it." Marilu felt so accepted by this group that she thought "I must be gay" and eventually tried gay sex. She began to believe that this was where she belonged.

IT'S TRUE!

◆ Roughly 80% of individuals involved in homosexual behavior come from homes where the father was a substance abuser or addicted to some other behavior.[1]

◆ Today there are at least 3,000 Gay/Straight Alliances (GSAs)—nearly 1 in 10 high schools have one—according to the Gay Lesbian Straight Education Network.[2]

transfuse (trans FYOOZ) *;* to cause to pass from one to another; transmit

The debates are ongoing: Is a person born gay or does he or she choose the lifestyle? Is homosexuality moral or immoral, normal or abnormal? These have become some of the most heated and controversial subjects in American society over the past decade.

The quick facts are found in the truth of God's Word, but let's first examine this behavior—where it comes from and how it might affect you as a student.

No temptation has overtaken you except such as is common to man; but God is faithful, who will not allow you to be tempted beyond what you are able, but with the temptation will

*also make the way of escape, that you may
be able to bear it.* —**1 Corinthians 10:13**

Most people will experience some type of sexual temptation. You can't turn on the TV, go to a movie, or walk the
mall without seeing and hearing about immoral sex. It's
there—it enters the mind. Add to this the brazen sexual
approaches of many students, both girls and guys, and
you have a great capacity for sexual temptation.

So is this temptation sin?

It is important to note the difference between *temptation*
and *conduct*. To experience sexual temptation is not the
same as acting on that temptation. It is not uncommon
to experience sexual temptation, because all of us have
a sin nature.

Temptation and lustful thinking are entirely different. You can be tempted to think lustful thoughts, but
you choose whether or not you will dwell on them and,
ultimately, act on them.

infuse (in FYOOZ) : to cause to be permeated with something
(as a principle or quality) that alters usually for the better

God does not condemn you for sexual urges, attractions,
or temptations—whether homosexual or heterosexual.
These come from our sinful nature just like the temptation to tell a lie, hide a fault to avoid punishment, or
selfish desires. Add to this the culture's attempt at nor-
malizing homosexuality, the militant gay agenda, and
the intense media and celebrity status given to the gay

lifestyle, and you will find your mind naturally affected by it all.

But the Bible clearly denounces immoral heterosexual and homosexual *conduct*. Lustful thoughts, both heterosexual and homosexual, are sinful behavior, whether you act upon them or not. Jesus said, "You have heard that it was said to those of old, 'You shall not commit adultery.' But I say to you that whoever looks at a woman to lust for her has already committed adultery with her in his heart" (Matthew 5:27–28).

So when does sexual temptation become a sinful, lustful thought?

It has been said that you cannot stop a bird from landing on your head, but you can surely keep it from building a nest there! Fleeting, unwelcome thoughts that you quickly and prayerfully dismiss are not the same as lustful thoughts that you keep in your mind and develop in your heart.

Consider honestly for a moment the sexual temptation you may be experiencing. How do your choices come into play?

+ Are there certain people, places, events, or habits that seem to encourage or bring about the temptations?

+ Are there certain people, places, events, or habits that empower you to have victory over the temptations?

Mark the following statements as true (T) or false (F):

_____ Sexual attraction is normal, and the influence of these attractions is a powerful force.

_____ Every believer has been given power over the sinful nature so that the constant suggestion and information need not degenerate into impure, sinful behavior.

BOTH of these statements are true! Remember, a repeated *choice* becomes a *habit*, and a repeated *habit* becomes a *lifestyle*. So be careful what choices you make about temptation!

THINK ABOUT IT

Are you experiencing the power of God over sexual temptation?

Playing with Fire

You may hear gay people say, "You straight Christians don't understand!" They might be right to a degree, but there are many Christians who have been delivered from the bondage of homosexuality and who do understand. Alan Medinger, a leader in the Christian ex-gay movement, proclaims his freedom from the gay lifestyle and writes, "When I look back and consider what might have been, compared to what my life is today, I can barely contain my gratitude."[3]

After twenty years of struggling with temptation, God set Alan free in a prayer time, and he has this to say about same-sex attractions:

1. *Attractions can lead to sin.* Many of us know from years of experience that our ventures into sin usually started with attractions to some person or some image. As James 1:14–15 says, "Each one is tempted when he is drawn away by his own desires and enticed. Then, when desire has conceived, it gives birth to sin; and sin, when it is full-grown, brings forth death."

2. *Attractions bring forth a painful longing.* This longing is not just a sexual desire, but rather a deeper longing for touch, affirmation, and intimacy.

3. *Attractions keep you from living the life you and God want you to live.* Constantly feeling sexually and/or romantically attracted to people of the same sex blocks this.[4]

Christ went to the cross so that you might be forgiven of sin and set free from its guilt, shame, and slavery. Think about this gift for a moment and the great price He gave for you. Why did He do this for you? Because He loves you and wants a blessed life for you.

Yikes! I Might Be Gay!

Teenagers who are dealing with sexual awakening that accompanies puberty and adolescence often ask, "If I have sexual attractions or feelings for someone of the same sex, does that mean I'm a homosexual?" The answer is no. Being attracted emotionally, romantically, or erotically to someone of the same gender is a complex issue with a complex mix of possible causes. Sue Bohlin says, "It really means that there are unmet, God-given needs for love and attention that were supposed to be met earlier in life. Having crushes on other people, of both sexes, is also a normal part of adolescent development. It means young people are transitioning emotionally from child to adult."[5]

Whatever the reasons, sometimes a young person is attracted to another same-gender person and may even act upon this attraction through engaging in homosexual or lesbian activity. This does not mean that the young person engaging in such activity is destined to be a homosexual. While young people may experience sexual identity confusion in their teens, the vast majority will turn out to be heterosexual in their behavior as they approach adulthood.[6]

Is There a "Gay" Gene?

Some in recent years have suggested that some people are born with a "gay" gene or with a genetic predisposition toward homosexual or lesbian behavior. In other words, their excuse is, "I can't help it; I was born this way."

In spite of intense propaganda by gay activists and other supporters of the gay cause, there is *no* evidence of a genetic predisposition to homosexual or lesbian behavior.

✦ Dr. Jeffrey Satinover, MD, a former Fellow in psychiatry and child psychiatry at Yale University, has demolished the so-called gay-gene evidence in his book *Homosexuality and the Politics of Truth*. Dr. Satinover's research concludes that there is no evidence, scientific or otherwise, of a genetic predisposition toward homosexual behavior.[7]

✦ In recent years, even some homosexual researchers and activists have acknowledged this truth. For example, homosexual researcher Dean Hauser says, "There is not a single master gene that makes people gay. . . . I don't think we will ever be able to predict who will be gay."[8]

✦ Famed lesbian author and activist Camille Paglia has said, "Homosexuality is not 'normal.' On

the contrary, it is a challenge to the norm. . . .
Nature exists whether academics like it or not.
And in nature, procreation is the single, relentless
rule. That is the norm. Our sexual bodies were
designed for reproduction. . . . No one is born
gay. The idea is ridiculous . . . homosexuality is
an adaptation, not an inborn trait."[9]

diffuse (di FYOOZ)' to pour out and permit or cause to spread
freely; to extend, scatter

The issue of being "born gay" could be debated forever
without a firm conclusion if feelings and emotions are allowed to be the only criteria. Many of those who live the
gay lifestyle believe that they have no choice in the matter and look at any suggestion otherwise as harassment
and hatred. Those who have been delivered by God from
homosexual sin now understand the truth and share the
story of God's grace and the freedom they have found in
Christ.

Melissa Fryrear has an amazing story to tell of the
grace and unconditional love of God. As her adolescent
years unfolded, she became aware that she was different
from other girls—she didn't like boys and didn't like being girly. So she thought, *I must be a lesbian.* At the age
of sixteen, she began her first lesbian relationship and
while in college joined the openly gay community. Then
Christ intervened in her life. Melissa's powerful story of
the Holy Spirit's "convicting revelation" can be found on
Focus on the Family's Web site and is guaranteed to be a
story you will want to share with others.

Melissa currently serves as gender issues analyst in
the Government and Public Policy office of Focus on the
Family. She will tell you from personal experience that
the journey to wholeness in Christ is one of repentance,
obedience, worship, and holiness.[10]

Melissa also reminds us that it is important to understand that for many homosexuals and lesbians, there are often deeply rooted issues that need to be worked through, oftentimes with the help of many people, professionals included, and that this process takes years. There is much to this journey. For example, a disproportionate number of women struggling with lesbianism have been sexually violated by a man and thus have a great deal of fear and distrust toward men. Likewise, many men have experienced a father's abandonment or rejection during childhood, and this may contribute to their intimate attractions. The same-sex feelings that these may experience as a result would not be sin.[11]

The Truth and Nothing but the Truth

Let's lay aside the emotions, temptations, and even scientific research as we now look at the plain truth of God's Word.

Both the Old and New Testaments speak clearly and unequivocally that homosexual *behavior* is sinful and contrary to God's plan for human beings.

+ God judged the wicked cities of Sodom and Gomorrah, known for their sexual perversions (Genesis 19:1–11).

+ "You shall not lie with a male as with a woman. It is an *abomination*" (Leviticus 18:22, 20:13; emphasis added). In this verse, the word *abomination* is the Hebrew word *tow`ebah,* which means "a disgusting thing."[12]

+ "God gave them up to *vile* passions" (Romans 1:26–27; emphasis added). In this verse, the word *vile* is the Greek word *ajtimiva,* meaning "dishonour, disgrace."[13]

+ "Do you not know that the unrighteous will not inherit the kingdom of God? Do not be deceived.

Neither fornicators, nor idolaters, nor adulterers,
nor homosexuals, nor sodomites" (1 Corinthians
6:9).

✦ The Bible perceives homosexual behavior as a
distortion of, and rebellion against, God's plan
for human sexuality. Thus, Paul says that for men
to have sex with men and women to have sex
with women is unnatural, or "against nature,"
and "shameful" (Romans 1:21–32).

Many gay rights groups have attempted to distort or
discount these Scriptures, but the Bible speaks clearly
about the subject. God's Word condemns homosexual
and lesbian behavior and is not in need of interpretation
concerning it. No matter what you may or may not feel,
it's ridiculous to say that your feelings are more important than God's Word.

Hebrews 13:4 says, "Marriage is honorable among
all, and the bed undefiled." Contrast the language
used to describe homosexuality to the blessing of God
pronounced on the marriage bed as *honorable.* What a
difference! Which will you choose?

Is Homosexuality Really That Important?
There are some modern apologists who argue for the acceptance of homosexual behavior within the Christian
community by saying that "since Jesus never mentioned
homosexuality," this issue couldn't be that important.
The answer to this frivolous and somewhat silly argument is several-fold.

First, the Old Testament condemns homosexual conduct in the most unmistakable terms (Genesis 19:1–11;
Leviticus 18:22; 20:13), and Jesus declared that He came
not "to destroy the law, or the prophets," but "to fulfill"
them (Matthew 5:17, 20).

Second, God created sex to make of a man and a
woman a "one flesh" relationship for life in marriage

(Genesis 2:18–25). Thus, any sexual relationship or activity outside of marriage is sinful. Jesus endorsed God's design for marriage as being between one man and one woman for life (Matthew 19:4–6).

Third, such assertions set up a false dichotomy between the teachings of Jesus and the writings of the apostles after His ascension into heaven. In fact, the resurrected Jesus declared to His disciples that it was better for Him to go to His Father because then the Holy Spirit would come in a new and mighty way. Through the Holy Spirit, Jesus would teach them many things that He couldn't teach them until the Holy Spirit came at Pentecost (John 16:7–15). The writings of the apostles in the New Testament epistles are the fulfillment of Jesus's promise. Consequently, there is no difference in authority in Jesus speaking in the gospel and Jesus speaking through the apostles in the New Testament epistles.

Can a Person Stop Being Gay?
Culture and emotions will probably say no, but the Scripture and the stories of countless thousands of former homosexuals tell us otherwise. Remind your friends or those who debate you that "with God, nothing will be impossible" (Luke 1:37).

Watch Out for Distortions

Often you will hear people distort the Bible to justify gay behavior. They may say that Paul's instruction to the Corinthians is referring to temple prostitution and the distortion of the homosexual lifestyle. They claim that a loving, monogamous gay relationship is not condemned in Scripture. Not true.

Writing to the Christians in Corinth, a first-century city noted for widespread homosexual behavior, Paul declares that among the "unrighteous" are the "effeminate" and the "abusers of themselves with mankind."

✦ effeminate (malakos) refers to the "passive partner in a homosexual relationship"

✦ abusers of themselves (arsenokoitai) refers to the "active member" in such a relationship

Paul attacks this modern-day argument with a detailed description of gay conduct.

God *can* change a person's heart towards sin, but it is not up to us to dictate *how* or *when* a person gives up a homosexual lifestyle. Remember that the Holy Spirit of God is powerful and that salvation is received in a moment of surrender and prayer; but the healing journey to wholeness takes time, because the emotional issues attached to it must be addressed and processed. Our call as Christians is to pray and care for others with the same patience and love that God shares with us and not to make demands or judgments. It is our privilege to walk patiently alongside those in the journey to wholeness with prayer and encouragement.

One thing we can do is offer the hope found in the words of the apostle Paul. He anticipated and answered the question of whether a person can find freedom from homosexual behavior in his letter to the Corinthians: "Such were some of you. But you were washed, but you were sanctified, but you were justified in the name of the Lord Jesus and by the Spirit of our God" (1 Corinthians 6:11).

There were Christians in Corinth who had been transformed and delivered from sexual perversion by accepting Jesus Christ as their Lord and Savior. Salvation changed homosexual behavior two thousand years ago, and it still can today! Why? *Because God's love is strong, His Word is true, and His Spirit is life transforming!*

For more great testimonies of people who experienced freedom from the homosexual lifestyle, visit www.exodus.to.

Help! My Friend Is Gay. What Do I Say or Do?
Christians are called upon to love and act redemptively toward people who are in a homosexual or lesbian lifestyle, but not to condone or accept their sexual conduct, which is clearly condemned by Scripture. How do we do this?

Love the sinner . . . *not* **the sin.**

♦ Explain that God created each of us with a unique purpose and plan.

Sexual immorality—whether heterosexual or homosexual—is not a part of God's plan.

♦ Compliment your friend on areas of life like: potential hobbies, interests, etc.

Life is about walking in the will of God in all areas of life, even when temptation makes it difficult.

♦ God demonstrates and speaks of His love for each of us throughout the Bible.

The Bible uses words like *against nature, abomination,* and *dishonor* to describe homosexual behavior.

♦ Invite him/her to church activities and secular, fun events that are neutral in the area of sexual behavior.

Don't try to go along out of curiosity or on a dare. You don't need to prove anything.

What is ONE THING you can do this week to show a person that you "love the sinner but not the sin?" Who is that person?

Before you go out to change the world, get ready!

+ *Pray.* Ask God for a compassionate heart so that you can share His love with others rather than just condemn them. Ask God to remove the sin in your own life, and be ready to share a testimony of God's forgiveness with others.

+ *Begin with compassion,* understanding that many of those in a gay lifestyle are blinded to the truth. Many homosexuals honestly feel they have no choice in the matter because they are sexually attracted to the same gender. By showing genuine unconditional love, you can show the truth of God's Word and allow the Holy Spirit to do the transforming work that only He can do.

+ *Know your stuff.* Don't use phrases such as "My friend/parent/church says it's wrong." "I heard it in church." "Everyone knows it." Have clear, easily understood Scriptures memorized and marked in your Bible to show to others.

+ *Stay true to God's Word,* even when tempted by emotion to do otherwise. Remember that emotion should not be the lead in choices you make, but God's everlasting Word should be.

+ *Look for ways to love people,* especially those who might make it difficult by their actions. Write a note, send an e-mail, offer to pray for needs, encourage, and always share personal spiritual blessings.

FUSE BOX

God created us with a specific purpose and plan in mind. Because He wants to bless us and wants the best for our lives, He has given us His Word to follow.

PRIVATE WORLD DEVOTIONS

MONDAY: See it. Read the surrounding passages or chapter for the Key Scripture so that you can get an understanding of the background and context. This helps you to really *see* the verse.

TUESDAY: Hear it. Read the daily Key Scripture and/or surrounding passage out loud, putting your name in, if applicable. For example, <u>John</u> *can do all things through Christ. Thieves have come to destroy* <u>John</u>, *but Jesus has come that* <u>John</u> *might have eternal life.*

WEDNESDAY: Write it. Write the verse and then what it says about:

+ *Others:* Respond, serve, and love as Jesus would.
+ *Me:* Specific attitudes, choices, or habits.
+ *God:* His love, mercy, holiness, peace, joy, etc.

PRIVATE WORLD JOURNAL

I am grateful for—I praise You for—I am feeling—I am thinking—I need help with

PRIVATE WORLD DEVOTIONS *(Continued)*

THURSDAY: Memorize it. Take the verse with you—write it on a card or put it in your phone, iPod, or PDA. Go over it throughout the day so that it begins to *live* in your heart and mind.

FRIDAY: Pray it. Personalize the verse as you pray for yourself or for others or in praise to God. To pray is literally "to think about." Try thinking out loud or writing in your **PRIVATE WORLD JOURNAL.**

SATURDAY: Share it. Ask the Lord to bring someone to mind or in your path today who needs good news. Don't be shy—just let it out! Whether you IM, write, text, tell, or send it, the joy of God's Word will flow from your heart into theirs.

PRAYER REQUESTS

Date	Name	Need	Answer

PRIVATE WORLD JOURNAL

I am grateful for—I praise You for—I am feeling—I am thinking—I need help with

NOTES

CHAPTER 7

WAR AND PEACE:
IS THERE A BIBLICAL "JUST WAR"?

KEY SCRIPTURE

*Jesus said to him, "'You shall love the L*ORD *your God with all your heart, with all your soul, and with all your mind.' This is the first and great commandment. And the second is like it: 'You shall love your neighbor as yourself.'"*
—Matthew 22:37–39

IN THE NEWS

Agnes Lackovic came to Germany from Slavakia as a teen in such ill health that physicians predicted she would soon die. The severely undernourished Agnes was taken in by her Aunt Rosa and given the hardy diet and medical care she needed to regain her health and start compensating for years of slowed growth. But her introduction to well-being didn't last long as Agnes found herself swept up in her aunt's dangerous work with the Munich underground forces.

In just three years, the undersized, but highly intelligent girl learned four languages—a capability that would assist Agnes in saving hundreds of lives during World War II. Her valiant efforts and ingenuity in coming to the rescue of scores of downed Allied airmen and captured soldiers ultimately earned her American citizenship after the war.

Hers is an amazing story of how one very ill and impoverished teen chose commitment and courage in the face of torture and death and helped save hundreds of lives as a result."[1]

IT'S TRUE!

+ Denied a childhood and often subjected to horrific violence, some 300,000 children are serving as soldiers in current armed conflicts.[2]

+ To avoid abduction by the Lord's Resistance Army (LRA), every night as many as 40,000 children in Uganda flee their homes in the countryside to sleep in the relative safety of towns. They seek refuge overnight at churches, hospitals, bus stations and temporary shelters before returning home again each morning. They are known as "night commuters."[3]

transfuse (trans FYOOZ): to cause to pass from one to another; transmit

Nightly news and talk shows debate the rights and wrongs of war, but both sides seem to have good points. So what's a Christian to believe? You're not the only one who is confused. Questions of *if* and *when* Christians may participate in armed conflict have plagued Christians since the first century AD.

In the first few centuries of the Christian faith, there were Christians who served in the Roman army (even in the emperor's guard). For example, a Roman military officer named Cornelius is portrayed in Acts 10 as a devout and pious man. Yet after his conversion we have no indication from Scripture that he refused to fulfill his military obligations. However, other early Christians practiced pacifism (the rejection of violence in all circumstances, including self-defense and defending others being victimized by violence).

By the middle of the fourth century AD, the question of whether Christians could participate in warfare became a critical one as a significant percentage of Roman citizens were becoming Christians. If large numbers of these new Christians embraced pacifism, then the Roman Empire would find it increasingly difficult to defend itself against its barbarian enemies.

One of the greatest early church theologians, St. Augustine (AD 354–430) attempted to address this question for the tens of thousands of new Christian converts. St. Augustine used an approach called "Just War" theory, which he adapted and revised from earlier Greek and Roman philosophers.

Augustine's Just War theory depended heavily on the teachings of the apostle Paul in the Epistle to the Romans. In the thirteenth chapter of Romans, Paul says that God ordained civil government in part to punish evildoers and that one of the tools available to administer such punishment is "the sword," a reference to lethal force. In other words, God authorized civil government to use lethal force to punish evildoers for domestic crimes and to protect citizens against foreign enemies.

> During the Arab–Israeli Six Day War in 1967, it was crystal-clear from aerial surveillance that the Egyptian, Jordanian, and Syrian armies and air forces were preparing to attack Israel. So Israel launched a preemptive strike that prevented their enemies from annihilating the state of Israel.

Consequently, from the early fourth century onward, most Christians in most places at most times have rejected pacifism and have acknowledged that resorting to military conflict by legitimate civil authority is justified under certain circumstances. Most Christians since the early fourth century AD have used some form of St. Augustine's Just War theory to determine if, and when, they are permitted to participate in armed conflicts.

*Jesus said to him, "'You shall love the Lᴏʀᴅ
your God with all your heart, with all your
soul, and with all your mind.' This is the
first and great commandment. And the
second is like it: 'You shall love your neighbor
as yourself.'"* —**Matthew 22:37–39**

Jesus keeps it simple—don't you love that? Life has so
many questions, and He brings us back to just two an-
swers: "love your God" and "love your neighbor". Com-
mentator Matthew Henry explains it like this: "*Love* is
the first and great thing that God demands from us, and
therefore the first and great thing that we should devote
to him. We must love our neighbour as ourselves, as
truly and sincerely as we love ourselves, and in the same
instances; nay, in many cases we must deny ourselves
for the good of our neighbour, and must make ourselves
servants to the true welfare of others, and be willing to
spend and be spent for them, to *lay down our lives for
the brethren.*"[4] As you read the criteria for what can be
termed a "just war," keep Matthew 22:37–39 in mind.
Honoring both God and man begins with love.

infuse (in FYOOZ) : to cause to be permeated with something
(as a principle or quality) that alters usually for the better

Just War theory is a form of moral realism—a reluctant
recognition that in a fallen and sinful world, armed conflict is, at least sometimes, the lesser of two evils.

The Just War theory:

✦ was never intended to justify war;

✦ tries to bring war under the rules of justice as understood by Christians;

✦ seeks to ensure that war, if and when it does occur, has limits and boundaries that at least limit its barbarity.

What are the Just War theory's commonly accepted criteria? After thirty years of study on this subject, Dr. Richard Land has put together a list of seven criteria for a "just war," based on the Scriptures and biblical principle.

JUST WAR CRITERIA

1. Just cause

Armed conflict is only permissible when necessary to resist and repel aggression and to defend those victimized by it. This does not mean that a country should wait to be attacked. In the modern world of technology, if a country has compelling evidence that an enemy is preparing to attack (marshalling its forces, positioning its planes and ships to attack), that government need not necessarily wait for an enemy attack before defending itself by the use of force. Having said that, please refer to the additional criteria and motives for a Just War defense:

✦ Only defensive war is defensible.

✦ The real, imminent threat of attack may justify a preemptive first use of force.

2. Just intent

The only acceptable motive for armed conflict must be to secure justice for all involved. Conquest, subjugation, revenge, or economic benefit are unacceptable, insufficient, and illegitimate motives for going to war.

The commandment "You shall not murder" (Exodus 20:13) remains God's law. However, there is a vast difference between murder and defending your family, your country, and your freedom.

3. Last resort

Resort to armed force can only be morally acceptable when all other reasonable avenues of resolving the conflict in question have been rejected or have failed.

As you hear people debate "just war" and how Christians should respond, ask the Lord to help you see people as Jesus does. He loves the unlovely, cares for the poor, and serves others. Ask yourself, "What would Jesus do in this current world situation?"

4. Legitimate authority

> *Therefore whoever resists the authority resists the ordinance of God, and those who resist will bring judgment on themselves. For rulers are not a terror to good works, but to evil. Do you want to be unafraid of the authority? Do what is good, and you will have praise from the same. For he is God's minister to you for good. But if you do evil, be afraid; for he does not bear the sword in vain; for he is God's minister, an avenger to execute wrath on him who practices evil.* **—Romans 13:2–4**

Paul wrote in Romans 13 that only the civil magistrate has the authority to use lethal force. For Americans, the duly constituted authority is the government of the United States. The way in which the American government authorizes military action is by a declaration of war or a joint resolution of Congress, however reassuring or helpful a United Nation's Security Council or General Assembly vote may be.

5. Limited goals

If the purpose of the resort to armed conflict is to resist aggression, to defend the innocent, to restore peace and to secure justice, then total annihilation of the enemy is never acceptable. Also, unless one's survival or freedom is in danger, Just War theory decrees that warfare is unacceptable unless the stated goals for the war have a reasonable chance of being achieved.

6. Proportionality

In other words, does the good gained by armed conflict justify the cost of injuries and loss of lives? Will the human cost of the armed conflict to both sides be proportionate to the stated objectives and goals? At what point is the good gained by warfare outweighed by the human costs expended in achieving it?

7. Noncombatant immunity

A war can only be just if it disqualifies noncombatants as legitimate military targets and seeks to minimize inadvertent civilian casualties. Making war on civilians is never justified.

Just prior to World War II, Dr. Land's father was with the United States Pacific fleet. If his naval task force had discovered the Japanese fleet (including several aircraft carriers) operating under radio silence a hundred miles from Pearl Harbor, they would have considered it an act of war. The US military could have ordered a preemptive strike on the Japanese fleet before it launched its surprise attack on Pearl Harbor, and possibly American involvement in WWII could have been avoided.

As you consider your position as a Christian committed to peace, think about this: Would you stand idly by if a gang attacked your mother, sister, or wife? What would you do? You would defend and protect immediately and not wait for the damage to be done.

As God calls you to stand on behalf of those in danger around the world, pray about your response and choices, which include:

+ serving as a chaplain, medic, or medical assistant;

+ serving as a soldier;

+ working with various peace organizations;

+ becoming involved in politics and helping to shape policy;

+ serving as a missionary in these areas.

Choose ONE THING you can do to make a difference:

❑ Commit to a regular prayer time for those in armed forces.

❑ Commit to write and encourage those in armed forces.

❑ Commit to a regular prayer time for the president and those in decision-making positions.

As you read this, you may be thinking, *If all parties accepted and lived by these Just War criteria, then there would be no wars, right?* Right! The theory's first test clearly states that no war may be justifiable unless it is a defense against an aggressor.

diffuse (di FYOOZ): to pour out and permit or cause to spread freely; to extend, scatter

Just War theory does not make war a good thing; it only allows for circumstances when war is sometimes a necessity. Because of the condition of fallen man, multitudes of people around the world are tortured, enslaved, oppressed, and impoverished.

✦ Through Just War, the human condition of fallen man can become less powerful and dominant.

> *Deliver those who are drawn toward death, and hold back those stumbling to the slaughter.*
> —Proverbs 24:11

✦ Armed conflict that meets Just War conditions is often much less terrible than the alternatives of enslavement or war unrestricted by Just War's limitations.

✦ These Just War criteria have stood the test of time because they are based on deep, underlying biblical truths.

If we see others being brutalized and victimized, we have an obligation to defend the innocent. God tells us that He will hold us accountable if we don't "deliver those who are drawn toward death, and hold back those stumbling to the slaughter" (Proverbs 24:11).

Jesus commanded Christians to love our neighbors as ourselves. He said:

✦ "You shall love your neighbor as yourself" (Matthew 22:39).

✦ "Whatever you want men to do to you, do also to them, for this is the Law and the Prophets" (Matthew 7:12).

If our nation were being attacked, we would want our neighbors to defend our families, our communities, and innocent civilians. As Christians, we should want for all people the minimum amount of violence necessary to restore peace and achieve justice for the greatest number of people possible.

> The true remedy for the war spirit is the gospel of our Lord.
> —Baptist Faith and Message

We must always remember that when lethal force is authorized by the state, it fulfills God's divine mandate to punish evildoers. So Jesus's teaching that we should turn the other cheek (Matthew 5:39) is referring to a personal decision not to defend oneself. It is an entirely different ethical decision than the decision not to defend one's neighbors when their lives are threatened by violent assault.

Most Christians have agreed over the centuries that we have an obligation to defend people who are being victimized and to participate in a government's defense of those victims through war, if the war meets Just War's causes, intents, goals, and restrictions.

For each Christian, whether or not to participate in war must be an individual decision, once the government authority has endorsed the use of armed force. Christians cannot abdicate their personal moral responsibility to the state. However, we must always render our ultimate allegiance to the Lord, not to the state (Luke 20:25).

Most Christians have found Just War's criteria extremely helpful in determining when, and under what circumstances, participation in the use of lethal force is morally justified. The decision to participate in a particular armed conflict is not a liberal or a conservative political decision, but a right or wrong moral decision.

War is a result of the sinfulness of mankind. Consequently, permanent and lasting peace will come only when Christ returns and subjects all powers to His authority. Until then, Christians must work for peace, contend for peace, and seek to avert warfare if at all possible.

FUSE BOX

For Christians, true peacemaking is to evangelize and proclaim the gospel of the Prince of Peace, Jesus Christ.

PRIVATE WORLD DEVOTIONS

MONDAY: See it. Read the surrounding passages or chapter for the Key Scripture so that you can get an understanding of the background and context. This helps you to really *see* the verse.

TUESDAY: Hear it. Read the daily Key Scripture and/or surrounding passage out loud, putting your name in, if applicable. For example, <u>John</u> *can do all things through Christ. Thieves have come to destroy* <u>John</u>, *but Jesus has come that* <u>John</u> *might have eternal life.*

WEDNESDAY: Write it. Write the verse and then what it says about:

- ✦ *Others:* Respond, serve, and love as Jesus would.
- ✦ *Me:* Specific attitudes, choices, or habits.
- ✦ *God:* His love, mercy, holiness, peace, joy, etc.

PRIVATE WORLD JOURNAL

I am grateful for—I praise You for—I am feeling—I am thinking—I need help with

PRIVATE WORLD DEVOTIONS *(Continued)*

THURSDAY: Memorize it. Take the verse with you—write it on a card or put it in your phone, iPod, or PDA. Go over it throughout the day so that it begins to *live* in your heart and mind.

FRIDAY: Pray it. Personalize the verse as you pray for yourself or for others or in praise to God. To pray is literally "to think about." Try thinking out loud or writing in your **PRIVATE WORLD JOURNAL.**

SATURDAY: Share it. Ask the Lord to bring someone to mind or in your path today who needs good news. Don't be shy—just let it out! Whether you IM, write, text, tell, or send it, the joy of God's Word will flow from your heart into theirs.

PRAYER REQUESTS

Date	Name	Need	Answer

PRIVATE WORLD JOURNAL

I am grateful for—I praise You for—I am feeling—I am thinking—I need help with

NOTES

CHAPTER 8

SALT AND LIGHT
THE RIGHTS AND RESPONSIBILITIES OF CHRISTIAN CITIZENSHIP

KEY SCRIPTURE

And He said to them, "Render therefore to Caesar the things that are Caesar's, and to God the things that are God's."
—Luke 20:25

IN THE NEWS

"I was seventeen when I first grasped what could happen in my life if I would simply trust God and believe what Philippians 4:13 says: 'I can do all things through Christ who strengthens me'. While attending Student Leadership University, I was challenged by Dr. Jay Strack to write down what my goals in life would be if I believed I had no limits. While I wrote many goals that some thought unreachable, one particular goal that stands out was my desire to be a national speaker for Students Against Drunk Driving. I was a leader in my high school's SADD chapter at that time, and I wanted to have an impact on the issue of alcohol use and abuse in this country.

For our citizenship is in heaven, from which we also eagerly wait for the Savior, the Lord Jesus Christ.
—Philippians 3:20

Even though I had set high goals and I believed I could reach them, my thinking was still limited in one way: I thought I could not reach these goals for many years. I soon learned that God does not have an age requirement. *He's ready to use us as soon as we start taking Him seriously.* Within one year, I had been selected to be the National SADD Student of the Year, where my primary role was to travel around the country speaking out on alcohol abuse. I met with the president to push for a national blood alcohol standard of .08. I also teamed up with New York's attorney general, Dennis Vacco, to end the practice of selling alcohol to minors over the Internet. I helped set up sting operations and lobbied Congress for federal legislation. We stood toe to toe with the alcohol industry—and we won.

During the past nine years, I have traveled to twenty-six states and three countries, speaking out on health and safety issues that affect my peers. I've had the opportunity to hold over forty press conferences, from the Capitol building to the White House, and I've appeared on news programs from NBC's *Today* show to CNN. I've met with President Clinton, lobbied Congress, and sat on the board of directors of three national nonprofit organizations that focus on alcohol use and abuse issues. After all this, I learned that bottom line is simple: young people can make a difference in the world if they will just open their minds to what God has planned for them." *(Nikki Finch, Program Director for Student Leadership University)*[1]

IT'S TRUE!

✦ Christians are more likely to register to vote than non-Christians.[2]

✦ Although Christians are most likely to discuss political matters with other people, they are the segment least likely to contact a political official to express their views on an issue.[3]

✦ Only 32% of non-Christian adults have a favorable impression of born-again Christians.[4]

transfuse (trans FYOOZ)*:* to cause to pass from one to another; transmit

The last seven lessons have handled some hot issues, and now that you know all this stuff, you may be asking, "What does it all have to do with me?" Everything. You have been called to an adventure-filled life, one that requires a dual passport. As disciples and followers of Jesus Christ, Christians are citizens in two realms—heaven and earth.

As citizens of heaven through faith in Christ, our ultimate allegiance is to Jesus and His kingdom. This can feel confusing in the light of conflicting government or cultural agendas. This conflict was also evident in Jesus's day, and they asked Him what to do. He gave them a simple answer: "Render therefore to Caesar the things that are Caesar's, and to God the things that are God's." (Luke 20:25).

Let every soul be subject to the governing authorities. For there is no authority except from God, and the authorities that exist are appointed by God. Therefore whoever resists the authority resists the ordinance of God, and those who resist will bring judgment on themselves. For rulers are not a terror to good works, but to evil. Do you want to be unafraid of the authority? Do what is good, and you will have praise from the same. For he is God's minister to you for good. But if you do evil, be afraid; for he does not bear the sword in vain; for he is God's minister, an avenger to execute wrath on him who practices evil. Therefore you must be

subject, not only because of wrath but also for conscience' sake. For because of this you also pay taxes, for they are God's ministers attending continually to this very thing. Render therefore to all their due: taxes to whom taxes are due, customs to whom customs, fear to whom fear, honor to whom honor is due. —**Romans 13:1–7**

What About Separation of Church and State?

The principle of the separation of church and state was never intended to mean the separation of religiously informed moral values from the nation's laws and public policy (Romans 13:1–7). As a practical matter, all governments must legislate morality in order to fulfill their God-ordained mandate to punish evildoers and reward those who do right.

God expects Christians to hold their government accountable to its purpose of punishing evil and protecting society. Laws making murder, theft, rape, and racism illegal are the legislation of morality. When Christians seek to make murder, theft, rape, and racism illegal, they are not so much trying to impose their morality on murderers, thieves, rapists, and racists as they are using the government to keep such perpetrators from imposing their immorality on their victims. This is not only the right of Christian citizens, but it is their responsibility and obligation.

When Christians seek to pass legislation protecting unborn children from being aborted by their mothers, they are not so much trying to impose their values on pregnant mothers as seeking to keep such mothers from imposing their immoral values on their unborn children, resulting in the death of these children.

A total separation of morality and politics is as harmful to moral values and public virtue as a complete dominance of a church by the state (or the state by the church) would be to all personal and religious freedom. The U.S. Constitution provides for a healthy balance in which the institutions of the church and state are kept separate, but individual citizens have the right to bring their religiously informed values to the debate on laws and public policies.

If Christians and other people of faith had been barred from bringing their faith convictions to bear on the public policy issues of the day, the nineteenth-century abolition of slavery and twentieth-century civil rights revolution would never have happened.

If Christians are obedient to the Lord's commandment to be salt and light, then we will be involved in both government and non-government efforts to right wrongs and alleviate suffering. We should be informed about the issues confronting our society, and we should vote in elections. And when we vote, we should vote our values, beliefs, and convictions, not merely our party loyalty or economic interests.

As Christians, even though our ultimate loyalty is to our heavenly Father, we live on the earth and have to obey the laws of our nation. Our testimony for Christ includes being good citizens by following the divinely given responsibilities and duties of earthly government "for conscience' sake" (v. 5).

God has ordained government to punish and restrict evildoers and to reward and protect moral behavior.

Can you think of a situation where there might be a conflict between the teaching of God's Word and the law of the government?

The question: *Where do I draw the line between God's law and the government's law?*

The answer: *Render . . . honor to whom honor is due.*

✦ Christians are commanded to support the civil state unless and until government requires Christians to support or do evil in direct contradiction to their ultimate allegiance to their heavenly Father.

Right now, the United States laws *allow* us to do things that are in direct contradiction to God's Word, but *do not require* us to do so. Do you understand the difference?

infuse (in FYOOZ)', to cause to be permeated with something (as a principle or quality) that alters usually for the better

Christians Have Obligations in Both the Spiritual and Earthly Realms

We are commanded to:

+ obey the law;

+ fulfill our civil obligations;

+ pay our taxes (Romans 13:1–7);

+ pray for those in authority (1 Timothy 2:1–2).

It is only when we are involved in society that we can preserve goodness and bring evil into the light.

Let's clarify: *involvement* is not the same as *imitation*. We are to be *in* the world, but not to be *of* the world. Got it?

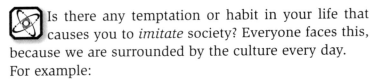 Is there any temptation or habit in your life that causes you to *imitate* society? Everyone faces this, because we are surrounded by the culture every day. For example:

+ We see immoral activities so often that they seem normal or permissible.

+ We hear certain immoral or unlawful arguments or offensive language until it becomes "white noise" rather than objectionable.

+ We may touch or be touched in dating situations and justify it as "not as bad" as others we know or movies we've seen.

✦ We might develop a taste for alcohol or other drugs if the culture's attitude toward these habits is, "Everybody does it."

Our families, our neighbors, our churches, our communities, and our nation are wracked by life-diminishing philosophies and values. Our society has been hit by a tidal wave of sexual immorality and a pornography-fed sexual violence against women and children both inside and outside their homes. Never before has America so urgently needed Christians to shoulder our responsibility to be *salt and light*.

SALT

You are the salt of the earth; but if the salt loses its flavor, how shall it be seasoned? It is then good for nothing but to be thrown out and trampled underfoot by men. —**Matthew 5:13**

✦ *Salt makes people thirsty,* so thirsty that they seek pure, living water, and lots of it. Jesus is that pure, living water, and He is the well that will never run dry. "Jesus answered and said to her, 'Whoever drinks of this water will thirst again, but whoever drinks of the water that I shall give him will never thirst'" (John 4:13–14).

> But the fruit of the Spirit is love, joy, peace, longsuffering, kindness, goodness, faithfulness.
> —Galatians 5:22

✦ *Salt preserves.* In a world that is increasingly drawn to evil, the salt of Christians preserves goodness and holiness. "He who now restrains [the Holy Spirit, working through Christians] will

do so until He is taken out of the way"
(2 Thessalonians 2:7).

✦ *Salt purifies.* Salt is used to clean, disinfect,
flavor, and purify. As "salty" Christians, we
can help others to find forgiveness of sin in
Christ, to be made new through salvation,
and to show a life of holiness. By sharing the
gospel, we can add "flavor" to those who have
no joy or hope in life. But Jesus warns us that
the Christian who seeks to be spiritual salt in
the world must remain pure. If the salt becomes
impure or contaminated, it is "good for nothing"
(Matthew 5:13).

How did Jesus act as *salt* in the world? List at least
three actions:

1. _____

2. _____

3. _____

Choose ONE THING you can do this week to be *salt* in a
way that Jesus was. Is there a specific place, person, or
event that you have in mind?

LIGHT

*You are the light of the world. A city that is set
on a hill cannot be hidden. Nor do they light
a lamp and put it under a basket, but on a
lampstand, and it gives light to all who are in*

the house. Let your light so shine before men, that they may see your good works and glorify your Father in heaven. —**Matthew 5:13–16**

✦ *Light removes fear from darkness.* The Christian who shows others the light of Christ offers peace and confidence to those he or she befriends.

✦ *Light exposes both evil and truth.* Those who walk in the light of God's Word show truth and expose evil.

✦ *Light gives hope and direction.* To know the light of Christ's love is to believe in a sure future and to have faith in His love.

> And this is the condemnation, that the light has come into the world, and men loved darkness rather than light, because their deeds were evil.
> —John 3:19

Jesus said, "I am the light of the world. He who follows Me shall not walk in darkness, but have the light of life" (John 8:12). This powerful Light of the World can only escape notice if we live in a way that denies the power of it. Light can cease to penetrate darkness if it is covered or obscured. As Dr. Martin Lloyd-Jones so aptly put it: "The true Christian cannot be hid, he cannot escape notice. A man truly living and functioning as a Christian will stand out. He or she will be like a city upon a hill, a candle set upon a candlestick."[5]

THINK ABOUT IT
Jesus said:

✦ "You are the light of the world" (Matthew 5:14).

✦ "I am the light of the world" (John 8:12)

Is this a contradiction? What do you think?

_____

_____

_____

Our Spiritual Obligations in the Heavenly Kingdom Combine with Active Involvement in the Earthly Kingdom
We do this, Jesus said, by being the "salt" of the earth and the "light" of the world. This commission by Jesus compels Christians to *active engagement with the world.* Preserving as salt and illuminating as light in a decaying and darkened world is not a passive, sightseeing trip.

diffuse (di FYOOZ)**:** to pour out and permit or cause to spread freely; to extend, scatter

- ✦ "Every Christian is under obligation to seek to make the will of Christ supreme in his own life and in human society and should oppose racism, every form of greed, selfishness, and vice, and all forms of sexual immorality, including adultery, homosexuality, and pornography."[6]

- ✦ Christians "should work to provide for the orphaned, the needy, the abused, the aged, the helpless, and the sick" and "speak on behalf of the unborn and contend for the sanctity of all human life from conception to natural death."[7]

- ✦ Ultimately, Christians "should seek to bring industry, government, and society as a whole under the sway of the principles of righteousness, truth, and brotherly love."[8]

Do you agree with these statements? Why or why not?

_____

_____

_____

_____

Is this asking too much of a Christian, or is this active involvement in the world a badge of honor?

> Though I speak with the tongues of men and of angels, but have not love, I have become sounding brass or a clanging cymbal.
> —1 Corinthians 13:1

_____

_____

_____

_____

If we read God's Word with understanding, we see that there are no areas of human society where Christians are not to penetrate as light and preserve as salt. It is an all-encompassing spiritual and temporal mandate.

However, expect that as you fulfill the *salt and light* commission, you will provoke a response from the world. Jesus did, and you will too. He said, "If the world hates you, you know that it hated Me before it hated you" (John 15:18).

If these words from Jesus teach us anything, it is that "to be a true Christian in all secrecy, comfortability, and enjoyability, is as impossible as firing a cannon in all secrecy."[9] Why? Because many in the world will find the salt irritating and the light bothersome.

Do you think you can stand against wrongdoing and cultural immorality even if it means being disliked or unpopular? Why or why not? What can you do to gain strength?

_____

_____

_____

Promises of Our Salt and Light Calling

Before you get discouraged, take great strength in remembering the other promises of Christ concerning your *salt and light* calling.

Jesus said, "Let your light so shine before men, that they may see your good works and glorify your Father in heaven" (Matthew 5:16). Yes, it is true that some will dislike and criticize you for your stand, but it is also just as true that some, even many, will come to know and

Lord, make me an instrument of thy peace,
Where there is hatred, let me sow love,
Where there is injury, pardon,
Where there is doubt, faith,
Where there is darkness, light,
And where there is sadness, joy.

Divine Master, Grant that I may not seek
To be consoled, as to console.
To be understood, as to understand;
To be loved as to love;
For it is in giving that we receive;
It is in pardoning that we are pardoned;
It is in dying that we gain eternal life.[10]
—St. Francis of Assisi

glorify Christ because of it! That is exciting and worth living for!

Love Overcomes All

Jesus spoke out against sin, but He unconditionally loves the sinner. We are obligated to do more than just vote for morality and righteousness in elections. We must live lives of radical obedience, giving ourselves in sacrificial service to others in Jesus's name. We must not only speak out in truth, but we must reach out in love if we are to influence others for Christ.

We can be faithful to this assignment as we:

✦ Love others with the love with which Jesus first loved us.

✦ Allow the divinely inspired, Holy Spirit-produced love that lives within us to savor the salt and energize the light that our Savior has called us to be.

Ask the Lord to put a person in your path this week who may be critical of your walk with Christ so that you can begin to show love to and pray for him or her. Is there anyone you already have in mind?

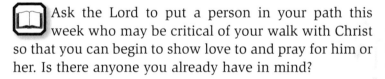

[**FUSE BOX**]

If we read God's Word with understanding,
we see that there are no areas of human
society where Christians are not to
penetrate as light and preserve as salt.

PRIVATE WORLD DEVOTIONS

MONDAY: See it. Read the surrounding passages or chapter for the Key Scripture so that you can get an understanding of the background and context. This helps you to really *see* the verse.

TUESDAY: Hear it. Read the daily Key Scripture and/or surrounding passage out loud, putting your name in, if applicable. For example, <u>John</u> *can do all things through Christ. Thieves have come to destroy* <u>John</u>, *but Jesus has come that* <u>John</u> *might have eternal life.*

WEDNESDAY: Write it. Write the verse and then what it says about:

- ✦ *Others:* Respond, serve, and love as Jesus would.
- ✦ *Me:* Specific attitudes, choices, or habits.
- ✦ *God:* His love, mercy, holiness, peace, joy, etc.

PRIVATE WORLD JOURNAL

I am grateful for—I praise You for—I am feeling—I am thinking—I need help with

PRIVATE WORLD DEVOTIONS *(Continued)*

THURSDAY: Memorize it. Take the verse with you—write it on a card or put it in your phone, iPod, or PDA. Go over it throughout the day so that it begins to *live* in your heart and mind.

FRIDAY: Pray it. Personalize the verse as you pray for yourself or for others or in praise to God. To pray is literally "to think about." Try thinking out loud or writing in your **PRIVATE WORLD JOURNAL.**

SATURDAY: Share it. Ask the Lord to bring someone to mind or in your path today who needs good news. Don't be shy—just let it out! Whether you IM, write, text, tell, or send it, the joy of God's Word will flow from your heart into theirs.

PRAYER REQUESTS

Date	Name	Need	Answer

PRIVATE WORLD JOURNAL

*I am grateful for—I praise You for—I am
feeling—I am thinking—I need help with*

Notes

CHAPTER 1—ABORTION: WHEN DOES LIFE BEGIN?

1. Testimony of abortion survivor Gianna Jessen before the Constitution Subcommittee of the House Judiciary Committee, 22 April 1996. http://www.abortionfacts.com/survivors/giannajessen.asp.

2. "Week Three," Stork Net. http://www.pregnancyguideonline.com/wk3.htm (accessed 21 July 2005).

3. "Abortion in the United States: Statistics," National Right to Life. http://www.nrlc.org/abortion/facts/abortionstats2.html (accessed 21 July 2005).

4. Strauss, Herndon, Chang, Parker, Bowens, Zane, & Berg. *Abortion Surveillance—United States 2001*. Centers for Disease Control and Prevention, 26 November 2004. http://www.cdc.gov/mmwr/preview/mmwrhtml/ss5309a1.htm (accessed 21 July 2005).

5. Ibid.

6. Tom Strode, "Bush urged to reject 'morning after' pill," *For Faith and Family News*, 15 January 2004, http://sites.silaspartners.com/partner/Article_Display_Page/0,,PTID314166|CHID596936|CIID 1843400,00.html?.

7. John Stamper, "Life in the Dark," Youth pamphlet © 2005. Used by permission of author.

CHAPTER 2—MERCY KILLING: DEATH ON DEMAND?

1. *Right to Life of Greater Cincinnati: Infanticide* (Ohio: Right to Life of Greater Cincinnati, Inc., 2003). http://www.affirminglife.org/issues/doe.asp.

2. Seth Mydans, "Assisted Suicide: Australia Faces a Grim Reality," *New York Times*, 2 February 1997, A3.

3. Lisa Allison, "Nitschke to Pick Recruits for 'Suicide School,'" *The Advertiser* (Australia), 30 November 2004, 25.

4. Euthanasia.com (2006), http://www.euthanasia.com/definitions.html (emphasis added).

5. Sarah-Kate Templeton, "Better for Old to Kill Themselves Than Be a Burden, Says Warnock," *The Sunday Times*, 12 December 2004.

6. C. Everett Koop, MD, *Koop, the Memiors of America's Family Doctor* (New York: Random House, 1991), http://www.nrlc.org/euthanasia/index.html.

CHAPTER 3—GENETIC ENGINEERING AND CLONING: WOULD YOU LIKE GREEN OR BLUE EYES WITH THAT?

1. Rita Rubin, "Early Genetic Testing Allays Fears, Ignites Ethics Debate," *USA Today*, 26 May 2004.

2. Joseph Carroll, "Society's Moral Boundaries Expand Somewhat This Year," The Gallup Organization (16 May 2005). http://poll.gallup.com/content/default.aspx?CI = 16318 (accessed 1 August 2005).

3. Jennifer Robinson, "Teens and the Future: Forecast vs. Fiction," The Gallup Organization (18 March 2003). http://poll.gallup.com/content/default.aspx?CI = 8008 (accessed 1 August 2005).

4. "How Cloning Works," www.usatoday.com, 6 February 2003.

5. Duke, Dr. Barrett, Director of the Research Institute of the Ethics & Religious Liberty Commission, on the release of the Institute's *Statement on Human Stem Cell Research* (26 October 2004).

CHAPTER 4—PORNOGRAPHY: IT'S JUST ONE LOOK, RIGHT?

1. Ian Kerner, *Help, My Son Is Hooked on Internet Porn*! Lifetime Television for Women. (2005). http://www.lifetimetv.com/reallife/relation/features/netporn.html (accessed 7 July 2005).

2. D. Kunkel, K. Cope, W. Farinola, E. Biely, E. Rollin, and E. Donnerstein (February 1999). "Sex on TV: Content and Context," The Henry J. Kaiser Family Foundation.

3. Linda Greenhouse, "Court Overrules Laws Restricting Cable Sex Shows," *New York Times*, 23 May 2000. http://www.nytimes.com/library/politics/scotus/articles/052300scotus.html (accessed 21 July 2005).

4. J. Peterson, K. Moore, & F. Furstenberg, "Television Viewing and Early Initiation of Sexual Intercourse: Is There a Link?" *Journal of Homosexuality*, vol. 21 (1991): 93–118.

5. Kaiser Family Foundation, 1996; 1998.

6. Richard Stengel, "Sex Busters," *Time*, 21 July 1986. http://www.time.com/time/magazine/article/subscriber/0,10987,1101860721-144566,00.html (accessed 21 July 2005).

7. "Porn in the USA," CBS News (5 September 2004). http://www.cbsnews.com/stories/2003/11/21/60minutes/main585049.shtml (accessed 21 July 2005).

8. *Baptist Faith and Message*, Article XVIII, "The Family."

9. Ibid.

10. *Final Report of the Attorney General's Commission on Pornography* (Nashville: Rutledge Hill Press, 1986), ix–xxvi, 31–48.

11. "Porn Not a Victimless Crime, Activists Say", www.cnsnews.com, 2 May 2001, cited in *The Issue: Pornography* (Nashville: The Ethics & Religious Liberty Commission, 2001).

12. William Barclay, *The Letters to the Philippians*, Daily Bible Study Series, rev. ed., (Philadelphia: Westminster, 1975), 79.

13. Ibid.

14. Ibid.

CHAPTER 5—TEEN SEX AND TECHNICAL VIRGINITY: HOW FAR IS TOO FAR?

1. John MacIntyre, "Facts of Life," *Spirit* (DFW Airport, TX: American Airlines Publishing, June 1999), 152.

2. Kaiser Family Foundation, *Sex on TV: A Biennial Report of the Kaiser Family Foundation*, 2001.

3. "A New Kind of Spin the Bottle," *Oprah*, 7 May 2002. http://www.oprah.com/tows/pastshows/tows_2002/tows_past_20020507_b.jhtml (accessed 8 July 2005).

4. *"Do You Really Know What Your Teen Is Doing?"* Oprah, 2 October 2003. http://www.oprah.com/relationships/relationships_content.jhtml?contentId = con_20031002_slang.xml&section = Family&subsection = Parenting (accessed 2 July 2005).

5. Gallup, 2002, cited in *LifeLight: Focus on Teen Purity* (Nashville: Southern Baptist Ethics & Religious Liberty Commission, 2003).

CHAPTER 6—TEEN HOMOSEXUALITY: CREATION OR CHOICE?

1. Bud Searcy, "Teens and Homosexuality: A Critical Time for Intervention," http://exodus.to/library_counseling_01.shtml (accessed 13 February 2006).

2. Gayteens.org, "News 24: Time magazine - Gay teen article," http://www.gayteens.org/714/modules.php?op = modload&name = New s&file = article&sid = 892 (accessed 13 February 2006).

3. Alan Medinger, "A Realistic Approach to Attractions," www.exodus.to.

4. Ibid.

5. Sue Bohlin, "Helping Teens Understand Homosexuality," http://www.probe.org/content/view/1192/72/.

6. Gary Remafedi, MD, MPH; Michael Resnick, PhD; Robert Blum, MD, PhD, and Linda Harris, "Demography of Sexual Orientation in Adolescents," *Pediatrics, the Journal of the American Academy of Pediatrics*, vol. 89 (April 1992).

7. Jeffrey Satinover, *Homosexuality and the Politics of Truth* (Grand Rapids: Baker, 1996), 109–17.

8. Traditional Vales Coalition Homosexual Urban Legend Series, "Sexual Orientation: Fixed or Changeable?" http://traditionalvalues.org/urban/seven.php.

9. Ibid.

10. Melissa Fryrear, "Love Won Out . . . And a New Seed Was Planted," http://family.org/cforum/pdfs/fosi/homosexuality/melissa_fryrear_bio.pdf.

11. Melissa Fryrear, personal correspondence to Diane Strack on 30 January 2006.

12. Brown, Driver, Briggs, and Gesenius. *The KJV Old Testament Hebrew Lexicon*, s.v. "tow`ebah." http://www.biblestudytools.net/Lexicons/Hebrew/heb.cgi?number = 8441&version = kjv.

13. Thayer and Smith, The KJV New Testament Greek Lexicon, s.v. "atimia." http://www.biblestudytools.net/Lexicons/Greek/grk.cgi?number = 819&version = kjv.

CHAPTER 7—WAR AND PEACE: IS THERE A BIBLICAL "JUST WAR"?

1. Agnes Lackovic Daluge and Willard Daluge, Rosa's Miracle Mouse: The True Story of a WWII Undercover Teenager, Authors' Direct Books; 2nd edition (January 15, 1999), http://www.jodavidsmeyer.com/combat/bookstore/WWII_teenager_rosa_miracle_mouse.html.

2. Human Rights Watch, "Stop the Use of Child Soldiers,"http://hrw. org/campaigns/crp/index.htm (accessed 13 February 2006).

3. Bruno Stevens, "The Night Commuters," Human Rights Watch, http://hrw.org/photos/2005/uganda/ (accessed 13 February 2006).

4. Matthew Henry, *Matthew Henry Complete Commentary on the Whole Bible* (1706), s.v. " Matthew 22." http://bible.crosswalk. com/Commentaries/MatthewHenryComplete/mhc-com.cgi?book = mt&chapter = 022.

CHAPTER 8—SALT AND LIGHT: THE RIGHTS AND RESPONSIBILITIES OF CHRISTIAN CITIZENSHIP

1. Jay Strack and Pat Williams, adapted from *The Three Success Secrets of Shamgar* (Health Communications, 2004).

2. "The Faith Factor in Election 2000," The Barna Group, 17 February 2000. http://www.barna.org/FlexPage.aspx?Page = BarnaUpdate& BarnaUpdateID = 46 (accessed 1 August 2005).

3. "Faith Has a Limited Effect on Most People's Behavior," The Barna Group, 24 May 2004. http://www.barna.org/FlexPage.aspx?Page = BarnaUpdate&BarnaUpdateID = 164 (accessed 1 August 2005).

4. "Surprisingly Few Adults Outside of Christianity Have Positive Views of Christians," The Barna Group, 3 December 2002. http:// www.barna.org/FlexPage.aspx?Page = BarnaUpdate&BarnaUpdate ID = 127 (accessed 1 August 2005).

5. D. Martin Lloyd-Jones, *Studies in the Sermon on the Mount* (Grand Rapids: Eerdmans, 1971), 1:174.

6. *The Baptist Faith and Message. A Statement.* Adopted by the Southern Baptist Convention (Nashville: LifeWay, 2000), Article XV, "The Christian and the Social Order."

7. Ibid.

8. Ibid.

9. Soren Kierkegaard, quoted in *Daily Devotional Bible Commentary* (Nashville: Broadman and Holman, 1974), 3:24.

10. Quoted in R. L. Middleton, *The Gift of Love* (Nashville: Broadman Press, 1976), 21.

ABOUT THE AUTHORS

Jay Strack, president and founder of Student Leadership University, is an inspiring and effective communicator, author, and minister. Acclaimed by leaders in the business world, religious affiliations, and education realms as a dynamic speaker, Jay has spoken to an estimated fifteen million people in his thirty years of ministry. His versatile style has been presented across the United States and in twenty-two other countries, before government officials, corporate groups, numerous professional sports teams in the NFL, NBA, and MLB, to more than 9,500 school assemblies, and at some one hundred universities. Zig Ziglar calls Jay Strack "entertaining, but powerful, inspiring and informative."

Princeton and Oxford-educated, **Dr. Richard Land** has served as president of the Southern Baptist Convention's Ethics and Religious Liberty Commission since 1988. During his tenure as spokesman for the largest non-Catholic denomination in the country, Dr. Land has represented Southern Baptist and other evangelicals' concerns inside the halls of Congress, before U.S. presidents, and as a presidential appointee to the U.S. Commission on International Religious Freedom (September 2001 to September 2004). He has recently been reappointed to the USCIRF by Senate Majority Leader Bill Frist to serve a third term. In February 2005, Land was featured in *Time* magazine as one of "The Twenty-five Most Influential Evangelicals in America." As host of a weekday radio program, *For Faith and Family*, Dr. Land is heard by more than 1.5 million listeners each week. An internationally renowned scholar, Dr. Land has worked tirelessly for the past two decades as a pastor, theologian, and public policy maker addressing our nation's social and cultural issues.

Lead, follow or be bait.

This is where the journey begins – SLU101!

At Student Leadership University, you won't find canoes and campfires. What you will find is a 4-day comprehensive program designed to catapult you into a life of confidence, significance, and leadership. SLU prepares you to successfully navigate the shark-infested waters of our culture with the rules and tools of leadership. Stop hanging out with the bait fish. Come to SLU where dreaming is encouraged and the language of leadership is spoken freely.

Explore the possibilities at
www.studentleadership.net

Student Leadership
UNIVERSITY®

We Believe in EVOLUTION.

Then   Now

...when it comes to radio.

Podcast

faithandfamily.com

with Dr. Richard Land